ENDORSEMENTS

"Dr. Estep has found a unique and creative way to explore the leadership traits of several biblical characters whose lives intersect with widely known servant leaders in Scripture. The study approach Eddie uses is worth exploring and makes the book even more valuable. Furthermore, the leadership lessons drawn from each story are excellent tools to help every person engaged in the leadership journey. Engaging reading!"

Gustavo Crocker
General Superintendent, Church of the Nazarene
Author, *Created for Mission*

"Many people can sing, but just a few know how to communicate a song. Many people can put words on a page, but a select few can actually reach into the reader's heart and mind. My friend Eddie Estep writes with a beautiful pen. I recommend his inspiring work to you!"

Bob Broadbooks
Regional Director, USA/Canada Region, Church of the Nazarene
Author, *How to Bless Your Pastor*

"What do you get if you mix the stories of King David with the wisdom of the Proverbs? You get the book *Who's By Your Side?* In a narrative world where people tell stories to make points, this is narrative at its proverbial best. Life lessons in leadership rise naturally from understanding the life and times of one of our story's greatest leaders, David. I also suspect that the author's own wisdom, gained in the trenches of leadership, has wormed its way into the pages. This is a great read."

Dan Boone
President, Trevecca Nazarene University
Author, *A Charitable Discourse* and others

"Eddie Estep has done it again. His previous book, *Who's Got Your Back? Leadership Lessons from the Life of King David,* was well received. This companion work, *Who's By Your Side? More Leadership Lessons from the Life of King David,* again draws on the author's years of leadership experience and brings the same helpful, storytelling, reflective approach to the narrative. Pastors and laity will find this book another helpful resource in the lifelong journey of developing as kingdom leaders."

Daniel Copp
Education Commissioner, International Board of Education
Global Clergy Development Director, Church of the Nazarene

"Once again Dr. Eddie Estep leads us into a great journey of study and praxis through the lives of those who have gone before. He reminds us that "great leadership requires competence and character." There cannot be one without the other, and the very lives of leaders must be infused with practical skills and the character that provides the backbone for what is very hard work. At the same time leadership cannot survive in a vacuum and must work to bring about the success of the entire team. The scriptural examples of relationship and team-building speak to us from history and provide us with a map into the future."

Carla Sunberg
President, Nazarene Theological Seminary
Author, *Reflecting the Image* and more

WHO'S BY YOUR SIDE?
MORE LEADERSHIP LESSONS FROM THE LIFE OF KING DAVID

BY EDDIE ESTEP

BEACON HILL PRESS
OF KANSAS CITY

Cover Design: Merit Alcala
Interior Design: Sharon Page

Library of Congress Cataloging-in-Publication Data
Names: Estep, Eddie.
Title: Who's by your side? : more leadership lessons from the life of King David / by Eddie Estep.
Description: Kansas City, Missouri : Beacon Hill Press of Kansas City, 2016.
  | Includes bibliographical references.
Identifiers: LCCN 2015038673 | ISBN 9780834135505 (pbk.)
Subjects: LCSH: Leadership—Biblical teaching. | Leadership—Religious aspects—Christianity—Textbooks. | David, King of Israel—Friends and associates.
Classification: LCC BS1199.L4 E88 2016 | DDC 248.4—dc23 LC record available at http://lccn.loc.gov/2015038673

The internet addresses, email addresses, and phone numbers in this book are accurate at the time of publication. They are provided as a resource. Beacon Hill Press of Kansas City does not endorse them or vouch for their content or permanence.

10 9 8 7 6 5 4 3 2 1

This book is dedicated to

those who faithfully stand by the side of pastors
and other Christian ministry leaders,
especially their spouses,

and to four Estep spouses: Diane, Brittany, Michelle, and Kim.
When your minister husbands are asked *Who's By Your Side?*
your names are the first mentioned.

——— ———

"Your words have put stumbling people on their feet,
put fresh hope in people about to collapse."
—Job 4:4, MSG

ACKNOWLEDGMENTS

My deep gratitude is expressed to those whose significant contributions have made this book possible.

Thanks to Bonnie Perry, Rene McFarland, Audra Spiven, and all the great people at Beacon Hill Press for their help and encouragement, and for modeling gracious perseverance during a challenging season.

Special thanks to Diane, the first reader of each chapter, for her many helpful comments, suggestions, and observations. Many thanks to Peggy Smith, the consummate executive assistant, for proofing and editing the first draft of the manuscript.

Much appreciation is extended to Geoff Kunselman, Joe McLamb, Steve Estep, Scott Estep, and Kim Duey, who read drafts of the manuscript and offered valuable comments and suggestions. If the book is helpful in any way, it is largely due to their contributions. Where the book falls short, I am solely to blame.

Finally, may God bless the friends, parishioners, and fellow ministers who stand by my side in the good times and bad. Your encouragement and examples make me a better leader and bring joy to the journey.

CONTENTS

FOREWORD

Though neither of us is native to the region, both Eddie and I have had the privilege of living in the southeastern United States. In addition to their sweet tea and love of all things barbecue, southerners are known for their speech. The combination of enchanting accents and colorful expressions makes listening a delight for outsiders.

I have come to realize that some southern idioms are nuanced. For example, "bless her heart" is not always as it first sounds. At times it is an expression of genuine sympathy, while in other situations it is nothing less than courteous derision. Another expression with more meaning than first meets the ear is, "I've been knowin' (name of person) (some extended period of time)." To the uninformed, this seems to be a mere statement of fact. However, I came to understand it is more an expression of admiration.

Well, (another good, all-purpose southern word), I've been knowin' Eddie Estep most of my life. We met as college freshmen who both expressed a call to preach. A friendship developed. We were in each other's weddings. We served two of the same churches. Later, when he became my overseer, I was privileged to be his family's pastor. We and our wives enjoyed many evenings cheering our kids (and occasionally "assisting" the umpires or officials) during high school basketball, volleyball, and baseball games. Mona and I always look forward to the next time we will be with the Esteps. We do a lot of laughing. Likewise, Eddie and I have been accountability partners, and thus shared our thoughts, feelings, disappointments, temptations, and questions.

Thus, I have had the privilege of knowing Eddie Estep both for a long time and "up close and personal." Life, being what it is, does not often allow for such. I have watched Eddie as a husband to Diane, as a dad to Josh and Jeff, and as a pastor and denominational leader. While Eddie's strength of discipline and never-ending desire to improve have led to his continued development, his foundation of impeccable character and love for God have been there as long as I have known him. In more recent years I have watched with satisfaction as others have come to recognize and appreciate his insights, leadership abilities, and gracious manner.

So when Eddie mentioned to me he was working on a book, I was not surprised that it would be proverb-like in nature. Both *Who's Got Your Back?* and now *Who's By Your Side?* are succinctly packed with wisdom. Many of the leadership lessons should be committed to memory and integrated into the fabric of one's soul so as to rightly display themselves as the situation, crisis, or decision necessitates. Likewise, the questions at the end of each chapter are useful for group discussions as we seek to "spur one another on" (Hebrews 10:24).

The serendipity for me of *Who's Got Your Back?* was its considerable value as a biblical reference. Thus, I came to anticipate such from *Who's By Your Side?*, and I was not disappointed. Even as a preacher of more than thirty years, I readily acknowledge my difficulties in remembering the many persons in King David's life, their interactions with one another, and how they fit into the bigger picture. These are the best books I have seen in putting David's people puzzle together.

So, if you are:

a military, church, business, or government leader;

a Bible student, teacher, or preacher;

a mentor, parent, or coach,

you will benefit yourself and those around you by reading *Who's By Your Side?*

Forewords are typically written by other authors or persons readily recognized. The purpose of such is to lend credibility to the book. It makes sense. I imagine publishers appreciate it for the sake of sales too. I am neither an author, nor is my name widely recognized. I know there are many others who could have been (and probably should have been) asked to write this foreword, and I am humbled. It speaks to the kind of person and friend Eddie Estep is.

Geoff Kunselman
St. Marys, Ohio
District Superintendent
Northwest Ohio District
Church of the Nazarene

INTRODUCTION

When Beacon Hill Press of Kansas City invited me to write a sequel to *Who's Got Your Back?*, I eagerly embraced the opportunity to explore additional characters beyond the twenty-six individuals covered in the first book.

The challenge was to discover and develop several more stories of individuals—friends, family, foes—with whom David has a significant relationship. Would there be enough? I was surprised by how easy it was to meet the challenge. The story of David is like a mother lode: The deeper you mine, the more treasures you find. For instance, it is amazing how many names are listed in the story of Absalom's rebellion alone, each serving as a reminder that in the midst of crisis, many individuals can contribute both to the problem and the solution.

The approach of *Who's By Your Side?* is similar to its predecessor, but there are a couple differences. This book, like the first, examines the dynamics of David's relationships and explores the leadership lessons from those relationships. Each chapter highlights a person who appears in the Old Testament account of David, examines the nature of that person's relationship with David, explores the leadership lessons revealed by that relationship, suggests questions for leadership development, and concludes with an excerpt from a psalm related to that chapter.

With regard to the differences, the first book begins with David's initial appearance in the Bible, his anointing by Samuel. This second book picks up later in David's story, at the beginning of his exile from Saul. The characters covered in *Who's By Your Side?* may not be as well-known as the characters covered in the first book. Do not be misled by what might be described as cameo roles in David's story. Though their appearances may be brief, their impacts are considerable. Some of the most important lessons leaders learn come from individuals who appear but briefly upon the stages of our lives but whose lines and actions leave indelible impressions.

During the writing, I was asked by a friend, "What is the big takeaway from this book?"

"The big takeaway," I responded, "is that great leadership requires both competence and character."

When David is at his best, he displays both competence and character. When he is at his worst, though he *sometimes* lacks competence, he *always* lacks character. Hopefully, you have by your side a friend of both competence and character. But if you cannot have both, avoid the temptation to value competence over character.

It is said of David in the New Testament that he "served God's purpose in his own generation" (Acts 13:36). If readers find within these pages encouragement to serve God's purpose in their own generation, with both character and competence, the prayer of this author will have been answered.

CAST OF CHARACTERS

Abiathar—son of Ahimelek; sole survivor of the massacre at Nob; serves as high priest during David's reign

Abigail—widow of Nabal; David's third wife

Abinadab—houses the ark of the covenant; father of Uzzah and Ahio

Abinadab—David's brother; Jesse's second son

Abinadab—son of Saul

Abishag—beautiful young virgin; serves as David's nurse

Abishai—David's nephew; brother of Joab and Asahel; son of Zeruiah; one of David's most trusted warriors

Abner—commander of Saul's army; Saul's cousin; murdered by Joab

Absalom—son of David; leads a rebellion against David; killed by Joab

Achish—Philistine ruler of Gath; provides sanctuary for David

Adonijah—son of David; challenges his brother Solomon for the throne

Adriel—husband of Merab; King Saul's son-in-law

Ahimaaz—son of Zadok; couriers vital intelligence to David during Absalom's uprising

Ahimelek—alternately spelled Ahimelech; priest of Nob who supplies David with bread and sword; murdered by Doeg

Ahinoam—Saul's wife

Ahinoam of Jezreel—David's second wife

Ahio—brother of Uzzah; son of Abinadab; helps move the ark of the covenant

Ahithophel—one of David's chief advisers; joins Absalom's conspiracy; grandfather of Bathsheba

Ahitub—son of Phineas; father of Ahimelek

Amasa—army commander for Absalom and David; murdered by Joab

Amasai—chief of the Thirty

Ammizabad—son of Benaiah; division commander for Israel the third month each year

Amnon—son of David; rapes Tamar; murdered by Absalom

Araunah—Jebusite from whom David purchases a threshing floor

Asahel—brother of Joab and Abishai; killed in battle by Abner

Baanah—brother of Rechab; together they assassinate Ish-Bosheth

Barzillai—leader of the three men who provide supplies to David and his men as they flee Absalom

Bathsheba—widow of Uriah; wife of David; mother of Solomon

Benaiah—one of David's elite warriors; Solomon's enforcer

Boaz—father of Obed; grandfather of Jesse; great-grandfather of David

Chileab—alternately spelled Kileab; David's second son; born of David's union with Abigail, widow of Nabal; surmised by many scholars to have died young

Doeg—an Edomite; Saul's henchman; massacres the priests and inhabitants of Nob

Eleazar—one of the Three mighty warriors of David

Elkanah—father of Samuel; husband of Hannah

Eli—spiritual leader of Israel; priest who raised Samuel; father of Phineas

Eliab—brother of David; eldest son of Jesse

Eliam—one of David's Thirty; father of Bathsheba

Gad—prophet who confronts David in the matter of the census

Goliath—Philistine giant; killed by David

Haggith—wife of David; mother of Adonijah

Hannah—wife of Elkanah; mother of Samuel

Hushai—friend of David; spy in Absalom's war council

Ichabod—name, which means "the glory has departed Israel," given to the grandson of Eli at his birth, in reference to the loss of the ark of the covenant

Ish-Bosheth—son of Saul; succeeds Saul as king of Israel

Ishbi-Benob—Philistine giant; threatens David; killed by Abishai

Ittai—Gittite commander in David's army

Jashobeam—alternate name for Josheb-Basshebeth in 1 Chronicles

Jedidiah—God's name for Solomon

Jehiah—a Levite; with Obed-Edom, has custody of the door to the ark of the covenant

Jehoiada—father of Benaiah

Jesse—son of Obed; father of David

Joab—David's nephew; commanding general of David's army; brother of Abishai and Asahel; son of Zeruiah; murders Abner and Amasa; slays Absalom against David's wishes

Jonadab—instigates Amnon's rape of Tamar; brings news of Amnon's death to David

Jonathan—son of Saul; friend of David

Jonathan—son of Abiathar; carries vital intelligence to David during Absalom's uprising

Josheb-Basshebeth—chief of the Three

Kerethites—mercenaries who, with the Pelethites, serve as David's special guard

Kimham—alternately spelled Chimham; son of Barzillai; enjoys David's favor

Kish—Saul's father

Maakah—wife of David; mother of Absalom and Tamar

Makir—one of three men who provides supplies to David and his men as they flee Absalom; provides accommodations for Mephibosheth

Malki-Shua—son of Saul

Mephibosheth—son of Jonathan; grandson of King Saul; lame in both feet

Mephibosheth—son of King Saul and his concubine, Rizpah

Merab—oldest daughter of Saul

Michal—David's first wife; daughter of Saul

Nabal—wealthy husband of Abigail; disrespects David

Nahash—Ammonite king; threatens Jabesh-Gilead

Nathan—prophet; confronts David over his sin with Bathsheba

Obed—son of Boaz; father of Jesse; grandfather of David

Obed-Edom—shelters the ark of the covenant in his home for three months

Paltiel—Michal (David's first wife) is given to him in marriage by Saul

Pelethites—mercenaries who, with the Kerethites, serve as David's special guard

Phineas—son of Eli; father of Ahitub; grandfather of Ahimelek

Rechab—brother of Baanah; together they assassinate Ish-Bosheth

Rehoboam—son of Solomon; succeeds Solomon as king of Israel

Rimmon—a Benjamite; father of Baanah and Rechab

Rizpah—Saul's concubine; her children are surrendered to the Gibeonites to be put to death

Samuel—last of the judges; first of the prophets; anoints Saul as king and David as king

Saul—first king of Israel

Shammah—David's brother; Jesse's third son

Shammah—son of Agee the Hararite; one of the Three

Sheba—leads a revolt against David

Shimei—curses David as he flees Jerusalem during Absalom's rebellion

Shobi—one of three men who provides supplies to David and his men as they flee Absalom

Solomon—son of David and Bathsheba; succeeds David as king of Israel

Talmai—king of Geshur; father of Maakah; maternal grandfather of Absalom and Tamar

Tamar—daughter of David; raped by her half-brother Amnon

Uriah—husband of Bathsheba; death arranged by David; one of David's Thirty

Uzzah—struck down by God for touching the ark of the covenant without being a Levite

Zadok—serves with Abiathar as high priest during David's reign; serves alone during Solomon's reign

Zebadiah—son of Asahel; commands 24,000 of David's men one month each year

Zeruiah—sister of David; mother of Abishai, Joab, and Asahel

Ziba—household servant of Saul; steward of Mephibosheth's property

— ONE —

AHIMELEK
SLAUGHTER OF THE INNOCENTS

The Background

The story of Ahimelek is told in 1 Samuel 21:1-9; 22:9-23; Psalm 52. He is also mentioned in 1 Samuel 23:6; 30:7; 2 Samuel 8:17; 1 Chronicles 18:16; 24:3; 24:6; 24:31.[1]

The Story

Before David reaches the age when many young men today graduate from college, he has already slain a giant, become a folk hero, achieved a high rank in the army, and married the king's daughter. But then King Saul grows insanely jealous of his son-in-law, and what has been a meteoric rise for David begins to closely resemble a falling star. After narrowly escaping Saul's two attempts at ending his life with a spear, it is only a quick-thinking wife and a fast exit that spare David certain death at the hands of Saul's goon squad, who have received orders to make David's wife, Michal (also Saul's daughter), a widow.

David becomes a man on the run. He flees to the tabernacle at Nob, fewer than three miles south of Gibeah. Lacking resources, David looks for food and a weapon, and will gain both from Ahimelek. Over his long career, many men will die in service to David, and Ahimelek will be among the first.

Ahimelek the priest is the son of Ahitub, the son of Phineas, the son of Eli.[2] Long after the death of Eli, priestly duties are still being carried out by Eli's great-grandson and eighty-four other members of the priestly family.

Apparently Ahimelek is afraid when David comes to him alone. It must seem strange that such a prominent man is unaccompanied. David probably appears weary and disheveled after his hasty flight for his life. Seeking clarification, Ahimelek questions David: "Why are you alone? Why is no one with you?" (1 Samuel 21:1).

David misleads him, telling him that King Saul has sent him on a secret mission. We do not know whether David lies for Ahimelek's benefit—so he will be ignorant of the conflict between David and Saul and thus protected from any charges of conspiracy—or for his own protection.[3] David's dishonesty hides from Ahimelek the risk he incurs by helping David, and in time, David comes to regret the deception.

David specifically asks for five loaves of bread or, if bread is unavailable, for anything Ahimelek can provide.[4] There is no ordinary bread on hand at the tabernacle, only the consecrated bread normally reserved for the priests. The tabernacle has a table that holds twelve loaves of consecrated bread, representing the twelve tribes of Israel. Each Sabbath, the freshly baked loaves are put on display in the sanctuary as a special, symbolic offering to God. The old loaves, after their removal, can be eaten—but only by consecrated priests.[5] When David requests the loaves, the priest declares that David and his men cannot eat the holy bread if they have been rendered unclean by sexual contact with women. David affirms that he and the men are ritually clean.[6] Thus pacified, Ahimelek agrees to bend the rules and hand over the bread.

David is not quite finished. He continues his pretense about the mission from Saul: "Don't you have a spear or a sword here? I haven't brought my sword or any other weapon, because the king's mission was urgent" (1 Samuel 21:8). Ahimelek reveals that a rare weapon is indeed on the premises—the massive sword of Goliath—and offers David the blade of the Philistine, which apparently has been placed in the tabernacle for safekeeping and as a reminder of God's blessing.[7] Now armed with the sword and provisioned with bread, David leaves Nob in peace.

The peace will not last for long, though. Unfortunately, Doeg the Edomite, Saul's chief shepherd, is nearby during David's exchange with Ahimelek and sees everything. He reports the meeting to King Saul, telling the king that Ahimelek provided David with guidance, food, and a weapon.

Saul then summons Ahimelek and all the men of his family who are priests at Nob. Under the tamarisk tree at Gibeah, with his spear in his hand, the king accuses Ahimelek of providing David with provisions and arms, of inquiring of the Lord for David, and of participating in what Saul perceives to be David's rebellion.

Ahimelek proclaims his innocence and ignorance of any kind of conspiracy.[8] He reminds the king that David is not only Saul's son-in-law but also his most trusted servant, and that Ahimelek lacked any reason to doubt that David had full authority to demand every favor Ahimelek granted. The priest's response is perfectly appropriate and reasonable.

Unfortunately, rational thinking will not sway Saul, for whom hysteria has replaced reason. The verdict Saul delivers is immediate and absolute: death. Death not only to Ahimelek but also to his entire family. Saul orders his guards to carry out the execution, but they refuse the command. Whether for moral considerations, concern for the king's sanity, or hesitation over violating the forbidden, the king's guards refuse to murder the priests of the Lord. It will take more than an impulsive command from the king to convince the palace guard to slay ordained priests.

Saul then orders Doeg to perform the execution, which the Edomite carries out with no hesitation. He murders Ahimelek and eighty-four of his fellow priests, along with all the inhabitants of Nob—women, men, children, and infants. With the exception

AHIMELEK

of one survivor, every living thing in Nob is destroyed, even the livestock.

The one priest who manages to escape the mass murder is Abiathar, son of Ahimelek, who brings the news of the massacre to David. Abiathar also manages to rescue the ephod—a priestly garment and tool of divination that will prove to be of great value to David.[9]

Leadership Lessons

1. You can tell a lot about people by where they go in times of trouble.[10]

When David first finds it necessary to flee Saul, in 1 Samuel 19, he turns to Samuel at Ramah. The next time he escapes Saul's murderous intent, in 1 Samuel 20, he turns to his best friend and Saul's son, Jonathan. Now, in desperation, he turns to Ahimelek, the priest at Nob. David shows a pattern of turning either to a covenant friend or to respected spiritual leaders.

Turning to the right person can be critical in times of distress. Trusted friends, wise advisers, and spiritual counselors can be helpful in the decision-making process and, as in David's case, the acquisition of resources for survival.

2. Religious rituals can either be obstacles to or opportunities for meeting human needs.

When Ahimelek is faced with the decision between honoring religious tradition and meeting human need, he determines that the law was given to advance life and that the spirit of the law demands that feeding the hungry should be prioritized over ritual if the two ever seem to conflict.

A thousand years after the death of Ahimelek, Jesus's disciples are seen walking through a field and plucking heads of grain on the Sabbath. They are accused by religious leaders of doing what the law of Moses forbade. Jesus responds to these enemies with a question: "Haven't you read what David did when he and his companions were hungry? He entered the house of God, and he and his companions ate the consecrated bread—which was not lawful for them to do, but only for the priests" (Matthew 12:3-4). Jesus cites Ahimelek's kindness to David as a precedent for subordinating the Sabbath and other worship regulations to the meeting of human needs.

Leaders are sometimes faced with situations that call them to make a choice between upholding traditions that safeguard religious ritual and providing help to the needy. When you find yourself in such a situation, let the examples of Ahimelek and Jesus be your guide.

3. There is sometimes a price to be paid for innocent kindness.

The massacre at Nob is bloody and senseless. Even though he is innocent of disloyalty to the king, Ahimelek pays a great price for his kindness to David. David is guilty of not making Ahimelek aware that David is asking for aid as a fugitive from the king, but Saul is guilty of destroying an innocent village.

The people who help you today may tomorrow pay a great price for the assistance they provided. Their kindness, and their sacrifice, should not be forgotten.

On the other hand, you may pay a price tomorrow for helping someone today. This risk should not necessarily dissuade you from acting on the opportunity to help someone in need.

4. There are people in this world who are "hopelessly committed to evil intentions."[11]

Saul's jealousy will lead to an obsessive focus on what he perceives to be a conspiracy to usurp his power. Saul is preoccupied with thoughts of his rival, even though in this account he carefully avoids referring to David by name.[12] Saul's paranoia is such that he will desperately grasp for power and control by implementing the extreme solution of massacring an entire village. It is the desperate act of a godless leader.

Throughout history, there have been leaders who have been equally committed to evil intentions.[13] But they almost never *start* that way. They often start out seeking to accomplish good but fall into the trap of trying to maintain power so they can continue to accomplish good. Maintaining that role soon becomes the single most important factor—even more important than accomplishing good—and the lengths they will go to maintain that power can be shocking.

Ironically, Saul's actions become so twisted that the actions God commanded Saul to take against the enemy Amalekites are instead carried out against Yahweh's priests at Nob—Saul's own people. Saul's intentions are evil, and when his guards refuse to act on his evil orders, he finds an equally evil and willing agent in Doeg.

5. If all those closest to you think your decision is wrong, you should rethink your decision.

Those entrusted with Saul's physical well-being (his guards) as well as those entrusted with Israel's spiritual well-being (the priests) know that Saul's decision to execute the citizens of Nob is legally unjustified and morally outrageous, and they tell him as much. Unfortunately, Saul is not to be dissuaded and presses on until he finds someone willing to carry out his orders.

If those closest to you, those who are most concerned about you, are convinced that your intended course of action is wrong, you would be wise to reconsider that course. Otherwise you, like Saul, may make a mistake of terrible consequence.

Questions for Leadership Development

1. To whom do you turn when you are in trouble?

2. What choice do you tend to make when faced with a decision between honoring religious ritual and meeting human need?

3. How should a follower respond when a leader's actions are malevolent?

4. What other leadership lessons can be derived from the story of Ahimelek?

The Psalm

John Wesley refers to David's "plain lie, extorted from him, by fear." Wesley also refers to Psalm 119:29, where David acknowledges his need for grace and "declares his repentance for this sin of lying."[14]

Psalm 119:25-32

I am laid low in the dust;
preserve my life according to your word.
I gave an account of my ways and you answered me;
teach me your decrees.
Cause me to understand the way of your precepts,
that I may meditate on your wonderful deeds.
My soul is weary with sorrow;
strengthen me according to your word.
Keep me from deceitful ways;
be gracious to me and teach me your law.
I have chosen the way of faithfulness;
I have set my heart on your laws.
I hold fast to your statutes, LORD;
do not let me be put to shame.
I run in the path of your commands,
for you have broadened my understanding.

— TWO —

JOSHEB-BASSHEBETH
DALEPH FORCE THREE

The Background

The story of Josheb-Basshebeth is told in 2 Samuel 23:8-17; 1 Chronicles 11:11-19. He is also mentioned in 1 Chronicles 12:6; 27:2.[1]

The Story

The Three are David's most prominent and revered warriors, honored above the rest of the soldiers of Israel. Josheb-Basshebeth the Tahkemonite is their team leader and chief.[2] The other members of this select squad are Eleazar, son of Dodai the Ahohite and Shammah, son of Agee the Hararite.

The Three are a special group within the Thirty. They are an elite unit of well-trained, battle-seasoned, highly decorated, incredibly effective warriors.[3] Though the criteria for membership are not listed, achieving heroic exploits against overwhelming odds is an obvious requirement. The Three are ancient Israel's equivalent to the U.S. Navy SEALs or Army Delta Force.[4] One major exploit is ascribed to each of the Three as they are introduced at the beginning of David's "Soldiers' Hall of Fame"[5] in 2 Samuel 23.

Josheb-Basshebeth is renowned for single-handedly killing eight hundred enemy soldiers in one battle, using only his spear.[6] Exactly how he accomplishes this is not disclosed, but that he does speaks volumes of his valor, ability, and stamina. The feat of rare courage and military prowess sets Josheb-Basshebeth apart and guarantees his place among the Three. This is, perhaps, the second-greatest individual exploit of war mentioned in the Old Testament, with only Samson's killing of a thousand men with the jawbone of a donkey being greater.[7] Josheb-Basshebeth later commands the twenty-four thousand men of the first division of David's army, who are on active duty in the first month each year.[8]

The Three also includes Eleazar, son of Dodai the Ahohite. Eleazar and David together taunt the Philistines who have gathered for battle at Pas Dammim. When the Philistine army advances against them, the other Israelite soldiers retreat in the face of the enemy. Eleazar, however, stands his ground and strikes down the advancing enemy until his hand grows tired and freezes to his sword as if it is welded there. Eleazar refuses to let go of the weapon until the battle is won. After the combat has concluded, the Israelite troops return to Eleazar—but only to claim the spoils of the battle.

The third member of the Three is Shammah, son of Agee the Hararite. Once again the Philistines have caused Israel's troops to flee. This time the Philistines are amassed in a field of lentils, threatening Israel's food supply. Shammah takes a stand against them, risking his life to defend the property and resources of Israel. Shammah stands alone in the middle of the field and strikes down the Philistines, keeping them from gaining the valuable field of crops.

Not only does the narrative in 2 Samuel 23 recount the individual feats of each of the trio of heroes, but it also records a combined exploit. The Three visit David when he is encamped in the cave of Adullam. The Philistines are positioned in the Valley of Rephaim and garrisoned in Bethlehem. It is harvest time, which probably means there has been no rain and the cisterns are empty. The dry conditions lead David to casually express a nostalgic craving for a drink of cool, clear water from the old well near Bethlehem that he used to drink from when he was a boy.

No orders are given, but none are needed to spur the Three to action. They are utterly devoted to David, and his wish is their command. Learning of the sentimental wish of their king, the Three immediately slip away to embark on a clandestine mission to gain the water for which David longs. They successfully breach the enemy lines of the Philistines, draw water from the well near the gate of Bethlehem, and return to David with the precious gift.

David is so touched by their effort that he cannot drink the water, feeling that to do so will cheapen the brave deed of the three heroes. For David, the water is hallowed, and represents the lifeblood of the brave men who have risked their lives to satisfy his desire. Instead, David pours out the water to the Lord as a sacrifice, as if to say, "This water is too precious for me to drink. Only God is worthy of such an offering." David's act acknowledges the sacredness of the devotion of these men and his own deep appreciation for their courage and loyalty.

Leadership Lessons

1. Stories of past struggles and victories can create the ethos and shape the identity of an organization.

Of all the adventurers, mercenaries, and fighting men who attach themselves to David, Josheb-Basshebeth and his two comrades-in-arms are among the greatest. They are models of courage and loyalty in David's army, and they readily follow his leadership. Stories of their bravery are told around campfires in reverent and hushed tones generation after generation. They are the kind of warriors that all the young men aspire to become.

Military units have long recognized the importance of stories of lore that mark a force and give them identity and pride.

Often those stories are distilled to a motto, slogan, or battle cry. "Remember the Alamo!," "Forty Rounds!" and "No Ground to Give!" are just a few of those slogans.[9]

Stories of bravery, courage, and sacrifice give a group identity, build morale, and provide motivation for continued acts of service and courage. Such narratives create an ethos and shape the identity of an organization. When the stories center around great hardships overcome through shared sacrifice, they achieve almost sacred status and become the foundation of *esprit de corps*.

Leaders are wise to identify such stories and learn to tell them often and well. Such narratives can define expectations, develop a culture of excellence, and inspire others to courageous and sacrificial service.

2. Leaders must sometimes stand alone, even if on a great team.

The Three are ready to stand together when able and willing to stand alone when needed. Josheb-Basshebeth, Eleazar, and Shammah each stand their ground against superior forces when other troops flee. Their brave stands prove to be the turning points that result in victories for Israel. Their examples bring to mind Martin Luther's words, "Here I stand."[10]

Heroic leaders stand firm even when everyone else runs in the opposite direction or when popular opinion trends the other way. A cord of three strands may not be easily broken,[11] but sometimes God helps a single strand to be sufficient for the task. No matter how intense the battle, no matter how weary the warrior, no matter how overwhelming the odds, heroic leaders stand their ground.

3. Some acts of bravery and service become sacrifices of which only God is worthy.

David's men honor him by courageously acquiring the water he craves and presenting it to him for his pleasure. Instead of drinking the water, David turns the cave into a temple and pours it out as an offering to the Lord.

Bill T. Arnold suggests that David's reaction "may seem ungrateful to modern readers." He further observes, "Instead of selfishly consuming water bought at such a great risk, David honors his men even more by offering it to Yahweh as a sacrifice."[12] Brueggemann memorably describes David's act as one of "sacramental imagination." Brueggemann explains,

> He [David] is able to discern immediately that this water, acquired at great risk and with the utter devotion of his men, has within it the bonding power of sacrament. Moreover David knows that to drink this water would be a violation of something holy that binds him to his men… David enacts a deep solidarity with his men by pouring the water into the earth, where none can abuse or possess the water. No wonder his men stood in awe of him, their devotion rewarded."[13]

We do not need leaders who are filled with selfish arrogance, who delight in personally benefiting from the sacrifices made by others. Leadership marked by selfishness and entitlement breeds discord. Self-renunciation produces loyalty, devotion, and unity. We need leaders who will gladly make such sacrifices because they prize "solidarity more than their own satisfaction."[14]

4. Leaders acknowledge when victory is the result of God's supernatural blessing.

Josheb-Basshebeth wields his spear against eight hundred men and wins. Such an accomplishment is only possible with the Lord's supernatural help. A victory of that scope is beyond human capability.

When recounting the individual exploits of the Three, the biblical narrative twice states that the Lord "brought about a great victory" (2 Samuel 23:10, 12). Brueggemann notes that in 1 Samuel 23:1 and 23:12, "the victories are credited to Yahweh, not to the soldiers or to David. The list reflects a powerful theological awareness."[15] Arnold also addresses this significant truth when he writes, "The narrator reminds us that the human perspective is inadequate to explain their successes… Even when celebrating the decorated war heroes, one must remember the source of their strength."[16]

Some leaders appear to be gifted with supernatural abilities in times of great challenge. It can be easy for those leaders to take the credit for victories that should be ascribed to God. Such leaders should be quick to acknowledge who ultimately determines the outcome of the battle and who gives the victory.

Questions for Leadership Development

1. What kind of a leader attracts men like Josheb-Basshebeth?

2. What character traits make the Three most admirable?

3. What stories of heroism and sacrifice need to be told in your organization?

4. How often do you, as a leader, deprive yourself of a benefit of your position for the good of the organization?

5. What are you doing to ensure that you are physically prepared for future opportunities that will require great stamina?

6. What other leadership lessons can be derived from the story of Josheb-Basshebeth?

The Psalm

Psalm 21 is filled with thanksgiving that God has granted success in battle and that his weapons have proven victorious. The psalmist gratefully acknowledges that it is the Lord who brings about victory.

Psalm 21:1-7

The king rejoices in your strength, LORD.
How great is his joy in the victories you give!
You have granted him his heart's desire
and have not withheld the request of his lips.
You came to greet him with rich blessings
and placed a crown of pure gold on his head.
He asked you for life, and you gave it to him—
length of days, for ever and ever.
Through the victories you gave, his glory is great;
you have bestowed on him splendor and majesty.
Surely you have granted him unending blessings
and made him glad with the joy of your presence.
For the king trusts in the LORD;
through the unfailing love of the Most High
he will not be shaken.

— THREE —

AMASAI
PICK YOUR PARTNERS CAREFULLY

The Background

The story featuring Amasai is told in 1 Chronicles 12:1-22.

The Story

Amasai, chief of the Thirty,[1] becomes a follower of David during David's exile. Some titles reflect such significance that further explanation is unnecessary; president of the United States, chief executive officer of a company, and coach of an athletic team are examples. In David's day, chief of the Thirty has a similar connotation. The title itself indicates that numerous exploits and achievements have qualified the individual for such a prestigious title. Such is the case with Amasai, "chief of the Thirty" (1 Chronicles 12:18).

While on the run from Saul, David attracts many followers who are willing to join his cause. The early comers tend to be men of broken fortunes and those who are distressed, discouraged, disgruntled, and looking for a place to belong. But as David's exile lengthens, he begins to draw a different class of men—daring and valiant soldiers who are attracted to David's lionhearted integrity. They recognize in David the qualifications of a national leader and are willing to transfer their allegiance to him.

In the season of David's exile marked by his sojourn in Ziklag and the wilderness stronghold, a steady stream of soldiers begins to arrive. These newcomers include three significant groups of warriors who join in rapid succession.

First, several men from the tribe of Benjamin unite with David's troops at Ziklag. These men are deserters from Saul's forces, even from Saul's own tribe. They apparently prefer the exile and reproach associated with David to the honor of Saul's court. These men are expertly trained warriors, well armed, and highly dexterous, gifted with the ability to shoot arrows or sling stones right-handed or left-handed.

Next, several Gadites defect to David while he is staying at his stronghold in the wilderness. These are courageous men, with the strength of resolve equal to great challenges—just the kind of men David needs. The tribe of Gad is situated on the far side of the Jordan, and the Gadites have shown their initiative and determination by crossing the Jordan at flood tide in order to join David. Only eleven are named, but they are men of great strength and exceptional training, disciplined military commanders fit for battle. Fierce in appearance and fleet of foot, the mere presence of these warriors spreads fear and puts a whole region to flight.

Amasai is the leader of the third group to join David. This company of men is from the tribes of Benjamin and Judah, and come to David in his stronghold. David himself goes out to receive them and challenge them, telling them that if they are coming with good intentions, they will be warmly welcomed. If, however, they have deception in mind, then God—who knows David's innocence—will judge them, because David's hands are "free from violence" (1 Chronicles 12:17).

One cannot blame David for initially suspecting treachery and wanting to be certain the men intending to join him will be loyal and trustworthy. David will not be reckless or heedless, for this is a matter of life and death. He is in supreme danger from Saul, and these men are not only from Saul's army, but they are also from Saul's own family tribe.

David speaks with candor and frankness, openly sharing his concerns. He is transparent and even acknowledges that he needs help. No doubt Amasai and the Benjamites find David's authenticity refreshing. He is willing to admit them into his service, but first he will put their intentions to the test. Wary and skeptical, David's words still reveal a willingness to trust: "If you have come in peace and to help me, you are most welcome to join this company; but if you have come to betray me to my enemies, innocent as I am, the God of our ancestors will see through you and bring judgment on you" (1 Chronicles 12:17, MSG).

Then the Holy Spirit comes upon Amasai, chief of the Thirty, who says,

We are yours, David;

We are on your side, son of Jesse.

Peace, peace be unto you,

And peace to all who aid you;

For your God is with you.

(1 Chronicles 12:18, TLB)

There is no hesitation in Amasai's response and no hint of offense at being questioned. It is as though he completely understands David's position and predicament. To allay David's fear of betrayal, Amasai pledges the wholehearted support of his group, acknowledging that God is David's helper. It is the speech of an articulate warrior—succinct, well spoken, and unwavering.

Amasai's reply satisfies David and gains his favor. David recognizes Amasai's sincerity and trustworthiness and hears in his words evidence of shared values and goals. Not only does David cheerfully accept them into his band of brothers, but he also makes them captains of his raiding bands. God first supplies David with men. Then God supplies David with leaders.

David's ranks continue to swell as more and more soldiers come his way: "Day after day men came to help David, until he had a great army, like the army of God" (1 Chronicles 12:22).

Leadership Lessons

1. When considering potential partners, leaders should clearly articulate their expectations.

When David receives Amasai[2] and his fellow men, his challenge to them implicitly contains these basic questions: *Can I trust you? Do you have my best interests at heart? Do you intend to help me succeed? Do you believe in what God is doing?*

David is not willing to accept the newcomers blindly. He will deal fairly with them, and he will do so by putting the matter to them. If they will be faithful and honorable, he will gladly receive them. If they are deceptive and will betray him to Saul, God will be David's avenger.

When Amasai responds by assuring David of their loyalty to him and by wishing prosperity and success both to David and to those who follow him, David is glad to welcome them to his cause.

Do not blindly accept people into your organization without giving them the opportunity to affirm their commitment—especially when accepting people into leadership positions. Ask the right questions—questions that will reveal their character in addition to their qualifications. Do not put out the welcome mat until your questions about their intentions and capacity for loyalty and devotion have been answered.

Pick your partners carefully in order to ensure that the right people are by your side.

2. Leaders know the difference between the ends and the means.

Amasai, chief of the Thirty, is a warrior's warrior. There is little question as to his ability to wage war. But war is not the focus of Amasai's speech. Amasai recognizes that the ultimate goal is peace. The noblest warriors most desire peace, not war. They recognize that war is sometimes the only avenue to peace.

The word *peace* is repeated three times in Amasai's concise response to David. He and his fellow warriors are ready and willing to fight, but they understand that the aim is not war. If they must fight, they will, but they will fight for the sake of peace. It is noteworthy that Amasai does not wish "victory" for David, but "peace"—reflecting an understanding that the goal is a unified nation, not a defeated foe.

Sometimes leaders confuse the difference between the mission and the methods. Leaders can be especially inclined to this error when their gifts and abilities are well suited to specific methods, and they sometimes make the main goal the employment of certain methods.

Amasai does not confuse the difference between the means (war) and the ends (peace). Neither should we.

Questions for Leadership Development

1. What are the dangers and opportunities of partnerships?

2. What qualifications should one look for in potential partners?

3. Why would people choose to follow a promising leader in a challenging situation over a poor leader in a comfortable situation?

4. What examples can you call to mind of leaders confusing the means with the ends?

5. What other leadership lessons can be derived from the story involving Amasai?

The Psalm

Amasai's wish for David is that he might experience peace. In Psalm 4, David testifies that following the Lord brings safety and peace.

Psalm 4:6-8

Many, LORD, are asking, "Who will bring us prosperity?"
Let the light of your face shine on us.
Fill my heart with joy
when their grain and new wine abound.
In peace I will lie down and sleep,
for you alone, LORD,
make me dwell in safety.

— FOUR —

ASAHEL
WHEN SPEED KILLS

The Background

The story of Asahel is told in 2 Samuel 2:18-32; 23:24. He is also mentioned in 2 Samuel 3:27-30; 1 Chronicles 2:16; 11:26; 27:7.

The Story

Asahel is David's nephew. He is the youngest son of David's sister Zeruiah, and the brother of Joab and Abishai. Asahel is honored as one of the Thirty. While Joab and Abishai ultimately become known for their military leadership, Asahel is known for his speed. He has the reputation of being "as fleet-footed as a wild gazelle" (2 Samuel 2:18).

Following the death of Saul, when war breaks out between the House of David and the House of Ish-Bosheth (the son of Saul), Asahel and his brothers fight for David's cause. When the opposing armies meet at the pool of Gibeon, each side selects twelve soldiers as representatives in hand-to-hand combat. The twenty-four soldiers killed each other, prompting a full-scale battle to break out in the civil war between David, who represents the kingdom and tribe of Judah, and Ish-Bosheth, who represents the kingdom of Israel.

David's men rout Abner and the Israelites, and Abner himself is put to flight by Asahel, who doggedly pursues him. As the swift Asahel begins to close the gap between them, Abner turns around and shouts, "Is that you, Asahel?" (2 Samuel 2:20). Asahel answers that it is. Continuing to run, Abner encourages Asahel to break off the chase and engage one of the younger soldiers in battle. Asahel refuses, continuing to narrow the distance between himself and Abner. A second time, Abner warns Asahel to break off his pursuit: "Stop chasing me! Why should I strike you down? How could I look your brother Joab in the face?" (2 Samuel 2:22). But Asahel continues his deadly chase, which proves to be his undoing.

Abner, the more seasoned and skilled warrior, suddenly stops, plants his feet, and thrusts the butt of his spear behind him. The maneuver is executed with the cold-blooded efficiency of a trained, experienced warrior. Unable to stop in time, Asahel impales himself on the blunt end of Abner's spear, which penetrates his belly and exits his back. He dies on the spot.[1]

As the battle rages on, those who happen upon the gruesome scene are overcome with shock, compassion, and grief at the sight of Asahel's body. The death sickens both sides and causes them to lose the heart to fight. As the day ends, Abner and his men hold a strong defensive position on the top of a hill. Abner calls out to Joab, suggesting a ceasefire, which Joab accepts. That day Abner loses 360 Benjamites who were fighting on his side. Including Asahel, only 20 of David's men are lost in the battle.

Some time later, Abner approaches David with the thought of uniting the kingdom under David's rule. When Joab learns of the meeting, he deviously summons Abner under the pretense of speaking with him confidentially. But the bitter Joab has murder in his heart and stabs the unsuspecting Abner in the belly, avenging the death of Asahel.

Leadership Lessons

1. Beware, lest your adversary use your strength against you.

Asahel is a renowned sprinter, but his greatest asset becomes the means of his downfall. Asahel's speed becomes a weapon that his opponent uses against him.

Asahel—one of the Thirty—is a considerable warrior, but he is no match for the wily, seasoned Abner. When Abner suggests that Asahel conquer a different soldier, Asahel refuses to consider a lesser prize. Even though Abner twice warns him, Asahel does not quit.[2] Asahel's ambition will be his ruin.

Leaders should recognize that their gifting in one area (such as Asahel's speed) does not equal a universal gifting in other areas (such as close-quarters combat). A common error among gifted leaders is to imagine that they are equally gifted in all areas.[3]

Abner is confident he has the experience necessary to vanquish Asahel. He knows he can outfight Asahel, even though he cannot outrun him. Some forms of self-defense, such as judo and aikido, use the opponents' own strength against them. Abner uses Asahel's strength of speed to bring about his demise. Asahel is swift of foot, an admirable quality in and of itself, but his swiftness leads to his premature, avoidable death. Ironically, Asahel could save his own life by listening to his enemy.

Do not let your signature strength become your enemy's secret weapon. The more prominent the gift, the greater the need for prudent wisdom in the use of the ability. Do not allow your enemy to turn your strength against you.

2. Beware, lest your momentum carry you to catastrophe.

Asahel is employing his speed effectively as he chases Abner. His forward motion, however, eventually carries him to a place he does not want to go—into the end of Abner's spear.[4]

Momentum is usually desirable. It allows organizations and individuals to make forward progress with greater efficiency. But it is possible for momentum to become dangerous if the pace becomes misdirected or reckless. Momentum can be hazardous in two situations: 1) when you are going in the wrong direction; and 2) when the momentum has become so breakneck that the ability to avoid danger is lost. When momentum reaches a frenzied pace, organizations and individuals lose the ability to react to changing conditions and respond to threats in ways that are timely and effective. It is possible for organizations and leaders, like automobile drivers, to overrun their headlights.

Do not let momentum take you places you do not want to go.

3. Beware the potential consequences of the action you are contemplating.

Both Abner and Asahel have the opportunity to weigh the potential consequences of their high-risk actions. Apparently, Abner knows Joab well enough to know that there is more than diplomatic relations at stake if Asahel is slain. Abner realizes it will mean trouble for him if he kills one of the sons of Zeruiah, and he hopes to avoid the blood feud that will result from striking down Asahel. After the deed is done, if Abner thinks the truce reached between himself and Joab will be permanent, he is badly mistaken. In retaliation, Joab murders Abner with help from his brother Abishai, against the wishes of David.

Asahel would know that engaging Abner in battle has the potential of high reward. Abner's capture or death will hasten the end of the war and ensure Asahel's fame. He would be well-served to consider more carefully the accompanying high risk involved in the encounter, for Asahel places his own life in jeopardy. Ultimately, Asahel's rash conduct leads to sad consequences. High risk can lead to great reward, but it can also lead to great loss.

Carefully considering the potential consequences of your contemplated action may spare you from an unfortunate fate. It is wise to consider as many eventualities as possible in order to prepare for potential consequences. Carefully weigh your high-risk actions to determine if the possibility of great reward outweighs the potential of great loss.

Questions for Leadership Development

1. How do you determine if high-risk/high-reward ventures are worth pursuing?

2. How do you determine which warning signs or voices to heed and which to disregard?

3. How can you protect against your strengths being used against you?

4. What other leadership lessons can be derived from the story of Asahel?

The Psalm

In Psalm 147, the psalmist contrasts the swiftness of the Lord (v. 15) with a lack of "delight in the legs of the warrior" (v. 10).

Psalm 147:10-18

His pleasure is not in the strength of the horse,
nor his delight in the legs of the warrior;
the LORD delights in those who fear him,
who put their hope in his unfailing love.
Extol the LORD, Jerusalem;
praise your God, Zion.
He strengthens the bars of your gates
and blesses your people within you.
He grants peace to your borders
and satisfies you with the finest of wheat.
He sends his command to the earth;
his word runs swiftly.
He spreads the snow like wool
and scatters the frost like ashes.
He hurls down his hail like pebbles.
Who can withstand his icy blast?
He sends his word and melts them;
he stirs up his breezes, and the waters flow.

— FIVE —

UZZAH
DOING THE RIGHT THING THE WRONG WAY

The Background

The story of Uzzah is told in 2 Samuel 6:1-11; 1 Chronicles 13:1-14.

The Story

The ark of the covenant is Israel's national treasure and most sacred object. It is the most valued and venerated symbol of Israel's faith and signifies the presence of God among his people.

The ark is a chest made of acacia wood, rectangular in shape, and covered entirely with gold, inside and outside. It contains three things: the tablets of stone on which the Ten Commandments are inscribed, Aaron's rod, and a jar of manna. Exodus 25 gives detailed instructions on how the ark is to be constructed.

Since the ark is built to be mobile, God gives specific instructions on how it is to be carried. Only members of a certain family branch within the tribe of Levi—the Kohathites—are allowed to carry the ark. They are told that "they must not touch the holy things or they will die" (Numbers 4:15). The ark is not to be touched by human hands. It is to be reverently carried on the shoulders of the Kohathites, using poles inserted through the rings attached to the ark. No matter how innocently it is done, touching the ark is in direct violation of God's law and will result in death.

For forty years, the ark accompanies Israel from Mt. Sinai to the Promised Land, and after they reach Canaan, it is housed first at Gilgal then in the tabernacle at Shiloh. When Samuel is a boy, the ark is in Shiloh, but the Philistines capture it in the battle in which Eli's sons are killed.

The Philistines soon learn that the ark is a dangerous thing. The people of Ashdod, where the ark is taken, are afflicted with tumors, there is a plague of mice, and the people are stricken with boils. The Philistines determine the ark to be the cause of their troubles and decide to return it to the Israelites—but not before some of their men dare look inside it, and seventy of them are killed. The Philistines grow so fearful of the ark that they place it and an offering on a cart, hitch up two milk cows, point them toward the border of Israel, and watch them go, unaccompanied.

When the ark reaches the border, it is taken to the house of Abinadab, where it remains for twenty years. Abinadab is the father of Uzzah and Ahio, both of whom will figure prominently in the history of the ark.

When David becomes king and establishes his throne in Jerusalem, he determines to restore the ark to a place of prominence by bringing it to the new capital. His action is designed to make Jerusalem both the political and religious center of the nation.[1] There the ark of the covenant will provide the focus for worship and serve as a rallying point for the nation.[2]

David confers with his military leaders, and the consensus is that it would be a good thing to bring the ark of the covenant to Jerusalem. The day David sets out to bring the ark to the capital city starts out as a very special day. Quite a crowd gathers at Baalah[3] in Judah for the momentous event. David assembles thirty thousand young, able men to serve as an honor guard in the procession that will bring the ark to Jerusalem. Significantly, thirty thousand is the number of Israelites slain when the ark is captured by the Philistines in 1 Samuel 4:10.

With considerable pageantry the ark is placed on a new cart pulled by a team of oxen and brought from Abinadab's house on the hill, with Abinadab's sons, Uzzah and Ahio, guiding it. Ahio is in the lead, walking in front of the ark, and Uzzah is walking beside it. David himself leads the procession, and all Israel joins him in worship—singing at the top of their lungs, accompanied by every kind of instrument they could round up.

The parade is going great until they reach the threshing floor of Nakon. Then things go horribly wrong. In one awful moment, the oxen hit some uneven ground and stumble, causing the cart to lurch. It looks as if the ark is in danger of falling off the cart. Uzzah instinctively reaches out to steady the ark, which is the last thing he ever does. He is immediately struck dead, and it is evident to all that God has done it.

As you can imagine, this sudden tragedy casts quite a pall over the festivities. It has about the same effect as a thunderstorm on a Rose Bowl Parade. David is badly rattled by the incident. First, he becomes angry, feeling more than a little embarrassed. In his humiliation, he blames God for the disaster. Then he grows fearful and decides to stop the proceedings. He orders a halt to the parade, sends everyone home, and places the ark in the nearest shelter, which happens to be the home of a man named Obed-Edom. For the next three months the ark is housed there, and during those three months it becomes evident that God is blessing that home.

Leadership Lessons

1. It is possible for leaders to cross the line.

Uzzah's punishment seems extreme without proper context. However, Uzzah crosses the line when he touches the ark of the covenant. Uzzah's intentions *are* good. He is trying to help. They need the ark moved, and Uzzah is more than happy to help. And who better? He has been around the ark all his life. He has grown up with the ark; it has been housed in his home for the last twenty years. Uzzah is also a Levite—a religious professional. He is one of the good guys.

In this case, familiarity may lead to presumption. Uzzah, having been around the ark in his own home for so many years, may have forgotten the holiness it represents. There may be times when we, too, fail to recognize the holiness of God, regarding him with an attitude of nonchalance. Uzzah may well have become so accustomed to the presence of the ark that he takes it for granted. Uzzah's death, therefore, is a means of preserving the sense of God's holiness and the fear of drawing near to him without appropriate preparation.

God is holy, and not to be trifled with, and if we are wise, we enter God's presence with that awareness. We do not utter God's name loosely or lightly, or profanely. We sing about God being a friend, but he is also a consuming fire and a fearsome presence.

Carelessness can happen to those of us who spend a lot of time around the church. There can be times when we fail to recognize the holiness of God. It is possible to become so familiar with God—and with the things of God—that we develop a careless attitude and forget the awesome, powerful majesty of his holiness.

There are some things in life that result in death. Touch a downed power line, and the result will almost always be instant death. Touch the ark of the covenant, and it means instant death. Commit adultery, and something dies. Trust. Faithfulness. Reputation. Lie or steal, and something dies. Trust. Credibility. Conscience. Cross the line, and something dies.

You may be familiar with C. S. Lewis's well-known series *The Chronicles of Narnia*. There is a famous line from *The Lion, the Witch, and the Wardrobe*. In the story the lion, Aslan, is the king of the beasts, the true ruler of Narnia, and—for readers—a symbol of Jesus Christ.

In the book, Susan asks about Aslan, "Is he—quite safe?"

Mr. Beaver responds with this now famous line about Aslan: "'Course he isn't safe. But he's good."[4]

God is certainly not safe. But he is good. He is holy.

Those who would draw near to God and have him draw near to them are those who approach him in reverence and holy fear. Uzzah forgets that lesson, and the consequences are tragic. When we forget, neglect, or take for granted God's holiness, we are in danger of crossing the line.

2. The great enemy of obedience is convenience.

Convenience is about saving time and effort; it's about making things easier, not harder. Convenience looks like a new cart and a team of oxen to transport the ark to Jerusalem. That method worked well enough for the Philistines several years before, when they returned the ark to Israel. That is probably what gives the Israelites the idea that the ark can be transported via oxcart. It is fast and easy and works just as well.

Or does it?

Obedience, on the other hand, looks like four Levite priests straining under the burden of carrying a heavy gold chest on their shoulders, supported by two poles. It looks like a ten-mile hike to Jerusalem, lugging a burden that will take several different people to accomplish.

It is a lot more convenient to carry a heavy object on a new cart, pulled by a team of oxen, than it is to carry it on your shoulders, with poles. David, Ahio, and Uzzah replace consecrated persons with a machine, using advanced Philistine technology. Machines are sometimes desirable because they do not require relationships and are not as messy or complex as people.[5]

There are many times when obedience is not convenient.

It is not convenient to pray. Prayer takes time, energy, and commitment.

It is not convenient to visit somebody in need of encouragement.

It is not convenient to practice evangelism.

It is not convenient to tithe.

It is not convenient to love your neighbor.

It is not convenient to feed the hungry, clothe the naked, house the homeless, or visit the imprisoned.

It is not convenient to bless your enemies.

It is not convenient to turn the other cheek.

No, these things are not convenient, but these are the things a holy God expects of a holy people. To do these things is to choose obedience over convenience.

3. God can take care of himself.

Uzzah, for a moment, feels it is his responsibility to save God. Uzzah, for a moment, believes that God almighty somehow needs his assistance. Uzzah, *in* a moment, discovers—fatally—that he is not responsible for saving God.

Life is not about our saving God; it is about God saving us. God does not need our help. God can take care of himself. God does not need us to save him. We need God to save us.

"God will not be put and kept in a box," writes Eugene Peterson, "whether the box is constructed of crafted wood or hewn stone or brilliant ideas or fine feelings… Uzzah has God in a box and officiously assumes responsibility for keeping God safe from the mud and dust of the world."[6]

You put God in a box at your own peril. When you have God in a box, it is easy to think you are in charge of God. We like to keep God in a box, and we like to live outside the box. It is usually a compliment to say someone is an outside-the-box thinker, that he or she is not confined by traditional thinking. But it is a dangerous thing to give God boundaries, while at the same time living without boundaries ourselves.[7]

4. The right things need to be done the right way.

The wisdom of moving the ark to Jerusalem is not in question. It is the right thing to do. Jerusalem—the political center of Israel—also needs to be the religious center. It is appropriate to relocate the ark. The issue is not *what* David determines to do; the issue is *how* David determines to accomplish it. One does not transport the ark the same way one would carry a load of turnips to market in Jerusalem.

The number-one pitfall of leadership may very well be doing the right thing the wrong way. The process is as important as the product. Leaders need to keep in mind that determining the right thing to do is only half the job. The other half is determining the right way to do the right thing. The means are as important as the ends.

Questions for Leadership Development

1. What is an area where you may be in danger of crossing the line?

2. How have you been tempted to choose convenience over obedience?

3. What does it look like when people put God in a box?

4. What other leadership lessons can be derived from the story of Uzzah?

The Psalm

Psalm 150 is reminiscent of the worship that takes place as various instruments are employed in praise when the ark is transported to Jerusalem.

Psalm 150:3-6

Praise him with the sounding of the trumpet,
praise him with the harp and lyre,
praise him with timbrel and dancing,
praise him with the strings and pipe,
praise him with the clash of cymbals,
praise him with resounding cymbals.
Let everything that has breath praise the LORD.
Praise the LORD.

— SIX —

OBED-EDOM
THE CYCLE OF BLESSING AND RESPONSIBILITY

The Background

The story of Obed-Edom is told in 2 Samuel 6:10-12; 1 Chronicles 13:13-14; 15:18-25; 16:5, 37-38; 26:4-8, 12-15. He is also mentioned in 2 Chronicles 25:24.[1]

The Story

Everything changes for Obed-Edom the day the ark of the covenant arrives at his house. Obed-Edom lives somewhere near the threshing floor of Nakon, along the route David takes to bring the ark of the covenant from the home of Abinadab to Jerusalem.

The ark comes to be sheltered at Obed-Edom's home due to a strange turn of events associated with the relocation of the ark. Parades with marching bands, a dancing king, thirty thousand soldiers, and a float featuring the ark of the covenant are not usual occurrences in Judah. Given the probable proximity of Obed-Edom's home to the parade route, his family must have great seats for the pomp and pageantry that occur that day. But then the oxen stumble, and Uzzah is struck down, stopping the parade dead in its tracks. The next thing Obed-Edom knows, a stunned and fearful King David requests that he shelter the ark in his home.

David's sudden fear, brought about by the divine punishment of Uzzah, may prompt him to approach Obed-Edom, who—as a Kohathite Levite—is a member of the family especially appointed to care for the ark. Whatever the reason that David entrusts him with the dangerous assignment, God is apparently pleased with Obed-Edom's treatment of the sacred chest. After only three months, we are told that God noticeably prospers Obed-Edom and his entire household.

It is not lost on David that God dispenses great blessing on Obed-Edom and his family while the ark is in his care. It is this blessing that convinces David that it is acceptable to bring the ark of the covenant into Jerusalem, provided it receives proper care.[2]

The ark is again transported, again with great rejoicing and fanfare, but this time the Levites transport the ark, as called for in Numbers 4:15. Once in Jerusalem, David has the ark placed in the tabernacle he has constructed for it.

Obed-Edom's service is not over the day the ark leaves his house, however. Those three months are only the beginning of what becomes a lifetime of service in association with the ark of the covenant. When arrangements are made for the celebration of the ark's safe arrival in Jerusalem and for its continued care, Obed-Edom figures prominently in both. His service continues in Jerusalem, where he is given more and more responsibility.

First, Obed-Edom serves as a musician assigned by David to minister before the ark when it is placed in the tabernacle. In 1 Chronicles 15:21 and 16:5, Obed-Edom is listed among the Levites whom David appoints to play lyres and harps to make a joyful sound with musical instruments in service before the ark.

Next, Obed-Edom is appointed as gatekeeper, which means he has the duty of controlling access to the tabernacle, in which the ark is first housed, and then to the temple, in which the ark later resides. Gatekeepers are Levites who have been entrusted with the role of protecting the Lord's house. They are in charge of the temple items, treasuries, and storehouses. In 1 Chronicles

26:15, Obed-Edom is given responsibility for the South Gate, and responsibility for the storehouse is assigned to his eight sons, who are described as "capable men with strength to do the work" (1 Chronicles 26:8). An examination of Obed-Edom in 1 Chronicles 26 makes it evident that he is experiencing a significant increase in responsibilities.

Finally, in what appears to be the pinnacle of his service in association with the ark, Obed-Edom becomes a doorkeeper. As a confirmation of his faithfulness, King David confers on him and Jehiah, another Levite, custody of the door to the ark. In 1 Chronicles 16:37-38, Obed-Edom "and his sixty-eight associates" are appointed as doorkeepers to minister before the ark, which is set inside the tent that David has pitched for it. The doorkeepers are the last line of human defense for the ark of the covenant. Posted at the threshold of the tabernacle, they are porters charged with protecting the sacred enclosures and guarding access to restricted places.

The doorkeeper is a very important and privileged job only entrusted to the most capable, loyal, and trained priest. The doorkeeper's job is to ensure that no one who is unclean or undeserving is allowed to enter the temple of the Lord. In this way, God's house will not be defiled.

God's blessing upon Obed-Edom is reiterated in 1 Chronicles 26:4-8, with the listing of his eight sons, who, with their own sons, are also active in service to the ark. In all, sixty-two of Obed-Edom's descendants minister before the ark.

The final mention of Obed-Edom occurs in 2 Chronicles 25:24. Long after his death, Obed-Edom's faithfulness and responsibility in safekeeping the ark and the gold and silver articles found in the temple are remembered in contrast to Amaziah's lack of faithfulness and responsibility. Jehoash, king of Israel, humiliatingly defeats and captures Amaziah, king of Judah, and takes the gold and silver articles found in the temple that were, so many years before, responsibly cared for and protected by Obed-Edom.

Leadership Lessons

1. Faithful leaders often experience cycles of blessing and responsibility, leading to increased blessing and increased responsibility.

The story of Obed-Edom is the story of a man who is given surprising, unexpected responsibility, which he handles well, and as a result, he is given additional responsibility. The presence of the ark itself is a blessing, but God's favor is not limited to that single blessing.

It may be providence that places Obed-Edom in the right place at the right time to initially take care of the ark of the covenant. But it is his faithfulness to that opportunity, and God's obvious blessing upon him and his family, that provide Obed-Edom further opportunities for increased responsibility and additional blessing.

Such a cycle of blessing and responsibility is often observable. Leaders are given responsibility. They faithfully fulfill that responsibility in such a way that blessings ensue. They are then given additional responsibility, which leads to additional blessings. The faithful, responsible service of a leader usually results in blessings, opportunities for greater service, and increased favor.

2. Responsible service can become a family affair.

Obed-Edom's sons and grandsons continue the family business. Obed-Edom considers the service to the people of God in the tabernacle and temple to be a family affair, providing a godly example for his many children, grandchildren, and other relatives—sixty-two in all, according to 1 Chronicles 26:8. Obed-Edom is put in charge of the South Gate, and his sons are keepers of the storehouse, but the favor and responsibility are also extended to Obed-Edom's grandsons.[3]

Obed-Edom and his family serve generation after generation as faithful gatekeepers in the temple, no doubt treasuring the stories of their family's long and loyal service to God's people. By his faith, attitude, and actions, Obed-Edom creates a heritage of service. In return, the Lord is gracious to establish for Obed-Edom and his family a legacy of generational blessings.

Your responsible leadership can lead to blessings for yourself and for your family. When faithful service becomes the family business, it can provide a legacy of generational blessings.

Questions for Leadership Development

1. How has the cycle of blessing and responsibility been evidenced in your own life?

2. In what ways has your faithfulness resulted in blessings to your family?

3. What other leadership lessons can be derived from the story of Obed-Edom?

The Psalm

Psalm 132, a song of ascents, highlights David's desire to bring the ark of the covenant to Jerusalem.

Psalm 132:1-9

LORD, remember David
and all his self-denial.
He swore an oath to the LORD,
he made a vow to the Mighty One of Jacob:
"I will not enter my house
or go to my bed,
I will allow no sleep to my eyes
or slumber to my eyelids,
till I find a place for the LORD,
a dwelling for the Mighty One of Jacob."
We heard it in Ephrathah,
we came upon it in the fields of Jaar:
"Let us go to his dwelling place,
let us worship at his footstool, saying,
'Arise, LORD, and come to your resting place,
you and the ark of your might.
May your priests be clothed with your righteousness;
may your faithful people sing for joy.'"

— SEVEN —

AMNON
FAMILY FEUD

The Background

The story of Amnon is told in 2 Samuel 13. He is also mentioned in 2 Samuel 3:2; 1 Chronicles 3:1.

The Story

Amnon is the son of David and Ahinoam of Jezreel. He is born in Hebron during the struggle between the house of David and the house of Saul. As David's firstborn, Amnon is heir to the throne. He occupies a privileged position based not on his own efforts but on the achievements of his father.

Amnon "falls in love with" (more accurately, begins to lust after) his attractive half-sister, Tamar, who is the full sister of Absalom. Despite his privileged position as crown prince, Amnon is powerless to have his way with his beautiful sister, and his raging desire becomes an obsession. Amnon becomes so tormented by his lust for Tamar that he makes himself sick with desire. Jonadab—Amnon's crafty cousin—observes Amnon looking gaunt and haggard, and inquires as to the cause. Upon learning of Amnon's obsession with Tamar, Jonadab devises a disgusting scheme to make it possible for Amnon to have the object of his desire.

It is a sinister and perverse plot. Jonadab advises Amnon to stay in bed the next morning. When David comes in to check on him, he should feign illness to the king (his appearance will corroborate the falsehood) and ask if Tamar can come in and fix him some dumplings ("special bread," in 2 Samuel 13:6) to aid his recovery.

David believes the lie, and Tamar is sent to cook for her brother. When she arrives, she proceeds to prepare and bake the dough, while Amnon ogles her from his bed. When the comfort food is ready, Tamar brings it to Amnon, but he refuses to eat. Amnon is not hungry for bread; he desires his sister. He makes everyone else leave the room and asks his sister to bring the food into his bedroom and feed him. When she does, Amnon grabs her and tries to seduce her.

Tamar responds with a firm refusal and resists Amnon's advances. But she is trapped and physically powerless to escape her brother, so she tries to reason with him, raising several objections. She highlights the moral impropriety and clearly identifies the consequence of what he intends, which is shame for both of them. Neither of them will have a future. It will disgrace her and discredit him. Tamar can clearly see the results of what Amnon proposes, but Amnon is blinded by lust. Amnon brushes aside her suggestion—which is probably a desperate attempt to buy time—that if he wants to marry her, David will probably agree.

Despite Tamar's resistance and pleas, Amnon does not spare his beautiful sister. He overpowers her and rapes her. The progression of his carnal desire has gone from attraction to lust to obsession to compulsion. The effects of the incestuous rape will be even more consequential than Tamar predicted.

As soon as the brutal act is done, Amnon's feelings for Tamar suddenly change. He is unable to stand the sight of the woman he has just raped. His lust turns into loathing—a vicious hatred that exceeds his previous desire for her. Now he abhors her, cannot bear to look at her, and wants her gone. He has a servant throw Tamar out of the house and lock the door behind her.

When Absalom hears what Amnon has done to Tamar, he begins to nurse a bitter grudge. Absalom refuses to speak to his brother and seethes with hatred for him. When David hears of the rape, he is furious but does nothing about it. He neither defends Tamar nor disciplines Amnon.

After two years, Absalom hatches a plot that has been simmering since the rape. The annual shearing of his sheep is an occasion for feasting and merrymaking, and it gives Absalom the opportunity to throw a party and set a trap for Amnon. All the king's sons, including Amnon, receive invitations to the sheep-shearing festival. Absalom even invites his father, the king, and his entourage to join them.[1] David graciously declines, saying his presence would create a hardship by overtaxing Absalom's hospitality. Absalom persists. If the king cannot attend, perhaps the crown prince can be the royal representative. The king declines again but then gives his blessing and permission for all the sons, including Amnon, to attend the event.

During the course of the party Absalom gives the prearranged signal, and his men rise up and murder Amnon, who may be too intoxicated to put up much of a defense. The reaction of the rest of David's sons is immediate. Suspecting a massacre, they take flight, making haste for the safety of Jerusalem in fear for their own lives.

The first report David receives is that Absalom has assassinated all of his brothers. At that news David becomes distraught. It is Jonadab—the late Amnon's adviser—who sets the record straight, sharing that only Amnon has been murdered and the rest of the king's sons are fine. He informs the king that Absalom has been plotting the demise of Amnon since the rape of Tamar.

Leadership Lessons

1. A leader's sins have the propensity to permeate the culture of an organization, institution, or family.

Everything changes for David and his family after David's tryst with Bathsheba and his murder of Uriah. David's sins—fornication and murder—create a climate in which it becomes easier for those sins to propagate. When leaders resign in dishonor after their immoral behavior has come to light, it is not uncommon for their successors to discover similar immorality throughout the organization. While a leader's sin may be hidden for a long time, it somehow infects the atmosphere of an organization, creating a toxic climate in which similar sins become rampant.

Almost imperceptibly, a leader's moral shortcomings can leaven the culture of an organization, institution, or family. Leaders would do well to consider that the full weight of sin cannot be determined immediately after the offense. The total effect of sin can often only be measured in light of generational impact.

The sins and shortcomings of the father are often reflected in the children.[2] Walter Brueggemann and Bill Arnold both note the parallels between the Amnon/Tamar story and the David/Bathsheba story.[3] Both Tamar and Bathsheba are off limits to the men who desire them. Like David, Amnon takes what is not rightfully his, and is willing to use force to get what he wants. The apple does not fall far from the tree.

2. When leaders encounter injustice, they can respond in ways that either end it or perpetuate it.

Unfortunately, the story of Amnon and Tamar points to the human condition. Acts of violence in which the strong take advantage of the weak are far too prevalent in our world.

Leaders with responsibility and authority have the moral obligation to seek justice and extend grace. We seek justice by ensuring that the perpetrators of violence and harm are held accountable for their actions. We extend grace by acknowledging that people have been wronged and by working for their restored health and wholeness. Our silence, however, like David's, often perpetuates the injustice.

Tamar does not receive justice, even from her own family. The ones who should serve as Tamar's support system instead become the ones who instigate and perpetuate the injustice. Her brother Amnon is the one who violates her. Her brother Absalom responds by trivializing Tamar's experience and counseling her to keep the matter to herself. If Absalom is waiting and watching to see what the king will do to punish the rapist, he is disappointed. David ignores the rape of his daughter.

Leaders have a responsibility to seek justice for those who are oppressed and not to ignore the wrongs suffered by victims of violence, injustice, or oppression. When we ignore the offenses inflicted upon innocent victims, our silence and inaction compound their suffering, and make it easier for injustice to spread.

3. Most moral problems, if ignored, breed further issues.

When David learns of Amnon's crime, the Bible says he becomes "very angry." But his anger does not result in action. He says nothing. He does nothing. He chooses to ignore the problem. Tamar is disregarded, and Amnon goes unpunished.

In the same way that Nathan spoke truth into David's life, someone is needed to speak truth into Amnon's life. That should be David, but he is too preoccupied. He may be paralyzed by the memory of his own sin. Perhaps it is hard for the father to discipline the son for the same kind of sin for which the father has been guilty.

For two years David ignores the problem. Then Absalom invites both David and Amnon to the feast he is hosting. David may have convinced himself that Absalom has forgiven Amnon. Absalom is indeed willing to bury the hatchet—directly into Amnon's head. The problem that David has chosen to ignore has now resulted in murder.

Leaders need the wisdom, discernment, and courage to appropriately address problems in a timely manner. When that wisdom, discernment, and courage are lacking, the problems often only multiply.

4. First reports are rarely entirely accurate.

The first report that David receives is that all of his sons have been massacred. David believes the news and is "beside himself," becoming distraught with grief. It is only later that the truth is revealed: Only one of David's sons has been murdered, not all of them.

In the stress of crisis, as in the heat of battle, first reports are rarely entirely accurate. The situation is seldom as bad, or as good, as first reports may indicate. A wise leader will seek additional information from reputable sources to determine the degree to which the first reports actually reflect reality.

Questions for Leadership Development

1. Why do leaders sometimes ignore problems they should be addressing?

2. How does a leader influence the moral climate of an organization?

3. What can a leader do to cultivate a healthy family environment?

4. What are the best ways for leaders to address injustice?

5. How do leaders build organizations (or kingdoms) to the detriment of their families?

6. What other leadership lessons can be derived from the story of Amnon?

The Psalm

Psalm 69 is the cry of a man whose family situation has become overwhelming. He acknowledges his own guilt and responsibility and concedes that he is a stranger to his own family. In his trouble he turns to God for deliverance.

Psalm 69:1-9

Save me, O God,
for the waters have come up to my neck.
I sink in the miry depths,
where there is no foothold.
I have come into the deep waters;
the floods engulf me.
I am worn out calling for help;
my throat is parched.
My eyes fail,
looking for my God.
Those who hate me without reason
outnumber the hairs of my head;
many are my enemies without cause,
those who seek to destroy me.
I am forced to restore
what I did not steal.
You, God, know my folly;
my guilt is not hidden from you.
Lord, the LORD Almighty,
may those who hope in you
not be disgraced because of me;
God of Israel,
may those who seek you
not be put to shame because of me.
For I endure scorn for your sake,
and shame covers my face.
I am a foreigner to my own family,

a stranger to my own mother's children;
for zeal for your house consumes me,
and the insults of those who insult you fall on me.

— EIGHT —

TAMAR

AM I MY SISTER'S KEEPER?

The Background

The story of Tamar is told in 2 Samuel 13. She is also mentioned in 1 Chronicles 3:9.

The Story

Tamar is the only daughter of David actually named in the Bible. She is the full sister of Absalom and the half sister of Amnon. Tamar is a striking princess and a virgin. Amnon finds her very desirable, but it is impossible for him to get near her. Perhaps the eunuchs keep careful watch over her, protecting her and keeping her safe from unwanted advances.[1] As a result, Amnon can do nothing about his lust but fantasize. He becomes so obsessed with Tamar that he makes himself physically sick with desire.

One day Tamar receives a message from her father, King David. The king has checked on his oldest son, Amnon, who is thought to be ill. Tamar is instructed to go to Amnon's house because he has not been able to eat and has specifically requested that Tamar be sent to fix dinner for him.

Tamar goes, as she is instructed, and begins to carefully prepare a meal. The account of her cooking preparations is descriptive: "She took some dough, kneaded it, made the bread in his sight and baked it" (2 Samuel 13:8). It is obvious that Amnon has plenty of opportunity to ogle his sister. This is not a meal quickly thrown together. It is a home-cooked meal, carefully and thoughtfully prepared for a sick brother.

When the meal is ready, Tamar places it on a platter to serve her brother. Amnon refuses to eat it. Instead, he clears the room of everyone else so it is just him and Tamar, alone. Then he asks her to bring the food into his bedroom and to feed him herself. When Tamar enters his room, Amnon grabs her and asks her to sleep with him. She says no.

Tamar raises several objections. First, she appeals to Amnon's sense of propriety, reminding him that such wickedness is not the way of the people of Israel. Then she appeals to his self-interest, pointing out that they will both suffer consequences—permanent disgrace for her and an irreparably damaged reputation for him. Finally, Tamar suggests that marriage is not out of the question.[2]

Her speech is impressive, articulate, and reasonable. But Amnon will not be reasoned with. Tamar's brother seizes her, overpowers her, and rapes her.

As tragic as the rape is, the story actually manages to devolve further. Amnon's treatment of Tamar after the rape is as brutal as the rape itself. Amnon suddenly hates the one he has desired so long and so intensely, and tells Tamar to get out. The social consequences of being banished seem, to Tamar, to be worse than the assault. A virgin violated and abandoned—even if she is the king's daughter—is considered unmarriageable, and is condemned to a lifetime of "desolation."[3] Tamar begs Amnon not to cast her aside, but Amnon insists on spurning her. He has a servant toss her out and lock the door.

Abandoned and forsaken, Tamar goes from the kingdom's most eligible bachelorette to the kingdom's least desired woman. By raping Tamar, Amnon has dehumanized her. Then he depersonalizes her, referring to her as "this woman" and refusing to call her name when he discards her.[4] By treating her as a divorced and shamed woman, Amnon only compounds a difficult situation. Kirsch observes, "No longer a virgin, Tamar was now unacceptable as a wife even if she was the daughter of a king."[5] Tamar regards herself as a woman beyond repair.

Now out on the streets, having been assaulted and devastated, Tamar cannot pretend that nothing has happened. She expresses her grief and mourning at the death of her dignity and her dreams. What has happened to her will be obvious to all who see her on the street, resulting in her private humiliation becoming public. Sobbing, her hands on her head, Tamar shows the cultural signs of mourning and distress, putting ashes on her head and ripping her elaborate, royal apparel.[6] The clothes that identified her as a virgin now publicly show her humiliation.[7]

It is worth noting that Tamar does not seek shelter in the palace of her father but in the home of her brother Absalom, who immediately recognizes what has happened. He counsels Tamar to hold her peace, and tries to comfort her by downplaying the incident. "Don't take this personally," Absalom advises. "After all, he is your brother, and not some stranger."[8]

Upon learning of the rape, David is angry, but he says nothing to Tamar and does nothing to Amnon. Strangely, David neither defends his daughter nor rebukes his son.

Once Tamar enters the house of her brother Absalom, she disappears from the pages of the Bible. Absalom preserves Tamar in memory by naming his only daughter—also beautiful—after her.[9] Two years later Absalom avenges the rape of Tamar by murdering Amnon.

Leadership Lessons

1. Anyone can become a victim of violence.

It is hard to imagine that there is any more privileged position in the kingdom than that which Tamar occupies. The beautiful, articulate daughter of the king, Tamar is dressed in finery, served by attendants, and admired by many. Her future is bright and promising.

That all changes the day she becomes the victim of Amnon's assault. Tamar's story mirrors the stories of many who have felt powerless and stigmatized as victims of violence.

Tamar is first victimized by the rape itself, and then her injustice is perpetuated by a society that allows a man to get away with rape, while a woman who is an innocent victim bears the shame and disgrace for the rest of her life.

Most distressing is the fact that, thousands of years later, this kind of injustice still happens. There are numerous stories—too many to count—of people who have been violated by family, friends, or strangers, scarred by the trauma of the experience, and then forced to bear the unfortunate and inappropriate rejection of friends, family, society, or the church. Many times women who have been raped are told they did something to cause that rape. The Bible makes no such judgment against Tamar. Amnon decides he wants her because she is physically attractive to him. Amnon plans, deceives, and uses his greater physical strength to overpower his sister.

Domestic violence is certainly a continued problem today. Family violence occurs on a daily basis in most of our communities. In *The Cry of Tamar: Violence Against Women and the Church's Response*, Episcopal priest Pamela Cooper-White argues that Tamar's story has a direct message for the church in its response to violence against women. Cooper-White elaborates on the different kinds of violence women often face, and critiques the church's response of forgiveness for the perpetrators at the expense of justice for the victim.[10] She concludes that the lesson learned from Tamar is that women and victims must be empowered with the full support of the Christian church.

The church is at fault if the only message is that of encouraging forgiveness. While that message is needed and necessary, it is inappropriate for the church's response to be limited in this way.

The church also needs to communicate a desire for justice for the victim, which includes ensuring that the perpetrator is not free to victimize others. The church should also seek justice for offenders, which involves holding them accountable for their actions.

2. Victims of violence need leaders who will listen to their stories, *believe* them, and take appropriate action.

Telling and hearing stories like this can be difficult. However, when such stories are untold and unheard, an atmosphere can be created where abuse festers and continues unchallenged. The rape of Tamar and the murder of Amnon are both violent, hateful acts. We need to acknowledge the fact that sometimes our stories—as individuals, families, and even as people of faith—are similar. It is important to tell Tamar's story because her story belongs to many people who are the victims of sexual violence.[11]

The suffering of victims is often compounded by the response, or the lack of response, of leaders. To ignore victimhood is to condone the crime that caused it. Victims need to be acknowledged, defended, protected, and nurtured toward health and wholeness. That process begins when someone is willing to listen.

The only reason we are able to read Tamar's story is that someone was willing to listen to her. Someone listened to the details, even though they were probably difficult to tell and difficult to hear. David does not listen. Absalom does not listen. But someone did.

The first step toward healing is being heard. It is often difficult for victims to tell their stories—because of pride, embarrassment, or a felt need for self-protection. Such transparency puts victims, once again, in a vulnerable place. Those who care enough to listen to such stories need to do so in the kind of setting and with the kind of sensitivity that creates a safe place.

The healing journey from abuse can be a lonely one. Victims may feel that no one else could possibly understand what they have been through and felt. When we listen to victims, and assure them that we believe them, we demonstrate that we value them as individuals and affirm their personhood. When we listen and believe, we acknowledge that victims deserve justice.

In many cases, once leaders listen, they will also need to take action, especially when they have the moral duty and positional authority to respond. Such action often includes immediate steps to safeguard the victim, reporting the alleged crime to the proper legal authorities, limiting the potential for additional harmful actions, gaining medical and/or psychological assistance for the victim, and initiating an investigation.

3. There are two kinds of family trouble: trouble from without and trouble from within.

All families experience trouble of some kind. None of us is immune or exempt from the problems and complications of life in a fallen world. The troubles families face can be broadly categorized as trouble from without and trouble from within.[12]

External troubles include problems like sickness, accidents, weather disasters, financial struggles, job loss, and relational problems with individuals outside the family.

Internal troubles include divorce, spousal or child abuse, domestic violence, selfishness, and relational friction inside the family.

Both kinds of trouble can be devastating for a family, but the more difficult of the two is trouble from within. The built-in support system of a family is compromised, and relational connections are jeopardized, when the trouble is from within.[13]

It appears that Tamar's family is more concerned with the reputation of the family, especially saving face for Amnon, than they are about the dignity of Tamar. Both Amnon and Absalom use David to suit their own purposes. Amnon is hungry for passionate pleasure and uses David to achieve his objective with Tamar. Absalom is hungry for political power and for revenge, and uses David to achieve his ambition. Both Absalom and Amnon are willing to satisfy their hunger in inappropriate and illegitimate ways.

In public, David is decisive, wise, and effective, but at home it is a different matter. Domestically, David is negligent and lax. His children are undisciplined, and David lacks parental control. He is too distracted to be a good father or a good husband.[14]

The rape of Tamar makes David angry, but he does nothing. If David truly has Amnon's best interests at heart, he would discipline Amnon. Love does not excuse criminal injustice and violence. Perhaps David does not discipline Amnon because to do so will open the family to public shame. Two years later, however, the public shame becomes worse. Incestuous rape gives way to fratricide.[15]

No one has Tamar's best interests at heart. Not her brother Amnon, who violates her. Not her brother Absalom, who silences her. Not her father, David, who ignores her.

Questions for Leadership Development

1. How would you respond to a friend or family member who had been a victim of violence (or how have you already done so)?

2. In what ways have you worked (or can you work) for justice for one who has been victimized?

3. What advice would you have for a family facing trouble from within?

4. What other leadership lessons can be derived from the story of Tamar?

The Psalm

Psalm 37 is a prayer of hope and faith for one who has been the victim of violence.

Psalm 37:9-15

For those who are evil will be destroyed,
but those who hope in the LORD will inherit the land.
A little while, and the wicked will be no more;
though you look for them, they will not be found.
But the meek will inherit the land
and enjoy peace and prosperity.
The wicked plot against the righteous
and gnash their teeth at them;
but the Lord laughs at the wicked,
for he knows their day is coming.
The wicked draw the sword
and bend the bow
to bring down the poor and needy,
to slay those whose ways are upright.
But their swords will pierce their own hearts,
and their bows will be broken.

— NINE —

JONADAB
BEWARE THE INSTIGATOR

The Background

The story of Jonadab is told in 2 Samuel 13.

The Story

Jonadab, the scheming and devious cousin of Amnon, appears in only two brief scenes, but his cameo role has considerable consequences for David and his family, as well as for the kingdom of Israel.

Jonadab, the son of Shimeah (David's brother), is "a very shrewd man" (2 Samuel 13:3). One day Jonadab, who is Amnon's cousin and adviser, notices Amnon moping around, looking haggard and gaunt. When Jonadab inquires as to the cause of Amnon's distress, Amnon shares his attraction to Tamar and desire to be with her.

Jonadab devises a cunning and vile strategy for Amnon to get his hands on Tamar. He suggests that Amnon pretend to be ill. Jonadab knows that David dotes on his eldest son and will be sure to come and check on him. Amnon is to tell his father, "I would like my sister Tamar to come and give me something to eat. Let her prepare the food in my sight so I may watch her and then eat it from her hand" (2 Samuel 13:5).

Amnon puts the plan into effect, and it reaps its intended results. As David instructs, Tamar dutifully presents herself at the house of Amnon to prepare his dinner. The making of the meal is described in detail. Then Amnon suddenly orders the others who are present to leave, and he rapes Tamar.

Jonadab disappears from the scene for two years. The next (and last) time he appears, he is in the king's palace. Word has reached David that his sons have all been massacred by Absalom. David's immediate response is one of intense grief and dismay. Jonadab assures David that only Amnon has been slain and that the rest of the princes are unharmed. Jonadab very coolly excuses the murder of his friend as retribution for the rape of Tamar. The king's sons soon arrive from Baal Hazor in a cloud of dust. As they dismount from their mules, Jonadab turns to the king and essentially says, "See? I told you so."[1]

The biblical record of Jonadab ends on that note. He is obscure—a minor character in a drama of intrigue, violence, rape, and murder—but the consequences of his instigation are clearly seen.

Leadership Lessons

1. Beware of those "eager to put their wits to the service of other people's evil."[2]

Amnon is apparently not enterprising enough to get Tamar on his own. But he finds a willing accomplice in Jonadab, who supplies him with a sordid and diabolical plan. Jonadab is able to get in on the action without getting his own hands dirty or being held personally responsible for what happens.

Jonadab's scheming ways do not end with the matter of Amnon and Tamar. One wonders how, two years later, Jonadab is at King David's palace at the right time to provide vital intelligence to the king. The enterprising manipulator is able to tell a grieving David that not all his sons are dead, only Amnon.

How Jonadab comes into this vital piece of intelligence is left unsaid. David would be wise to ask, "How did you get this information, Jonadab? And why have you not revealed it until now?"

The most likely way for Jonadab to know what happened in Baal Hazor—even before accurate firsthand reports reach Jerusalem—is that Jonadab has been complicit in the conspiracy. He may have been involved in the scheme from its inception. Absalom may have even planted him in David's household to provide information that will keep David from taking immediate steps to neutralize Absalom's threat to the throne. Perhaps Jonadab hopes for a future appointment to Absalom's cabinet in return.

Modern-day Jonadabs can be found all over the world. They are dedicated to helping men and women satisfy their evil desires.[3] These individuals often use modern-day means and contemporary technology to advance the ancient craft of disseminating sordid, diabolical suggestions and propagating reprehensible advice.

There will often be a Jonadab who will try to get close to a leader and eagerly legitimize a leader's illegitimate emotions and desires. What makes these folks so dangerous to leaders is that they *do* provide useful information. And, at times, leaders may have trouble determining if a person seems to be always near the scene of the crime because they are instigating crimes or because they are actively trying to prevent crimes.[4]

Beware of instigators.

2. The character of the adviser is often indicative of the quality of the advice.

This whole, sordid story begins because Amnon listens to bad advice. Ever looking for an opportunity to ingratiate himself with the man who will one day be king, Jonadab guises himself in a cloak of concern when he observes Amnon's anxious, disheveled appearance. He no doubt believes that helping Amnon get what he wants will result in Jonadab getting what *he* wants—the perks and power associated with being in the future king's inner circle.

Jonadab's deceitful plan is only a reflection of what is in his heart. Deceiving David and violating Tamar are deemed justifiable if the result is Amnon's satisfaction.

The character of your friends is often indicative of the quality of their advice. Leaders can quickly get themselves in trouble by selecting advisers based on *competence* alone, without considering *character*. The fruit of Jonadab's bad character is bad advice. A generation later, Rehoboam, the son of Solomon, will also seek advice from the wrong kind of friends.[5] The consequences of that advice, like Jonadab's, will prove devastating.

Leaders need advisers with good character. Such advisers can offer counsel that has the best interests of the organization in mind, rather than guidance that has the best interests of the adviser in mind.

If the advice you receive comes from a person of bad character, you would be wise to reconsider before implementing that person's advice. If the advice you receive entails the deception or violation of another, you would be wise to completely ignore that person's advice.

The kind of advice you seek also reveals your own character. You can always find someone who will validate your desires and tell you what you want to hear. Only strong leaders value truth more than the validation of their own opinions and desires.[6]

Beware of counsel offered by persons of bad character, for the fruit of bad character is bad advice.

Questions for Leadership Development

1. How do you decide who will be your adviser?

2. How do you determine the quality of the advice you receive?

3. How do you discern whether someone in your circle of influence is an instigator whose advice you should not heed?

4. What other leadership lessons can be derived from the story of Jonadab?

The Psalm

Psalm 64 contains David's prayer that God would safeguard him from the plots and plans of those with harmful intentions.

Psalm 64:1-8

Hear me, my God, as I voice my complaint;
protect my life from the threat of the enemy.
Hide me from the conspiracy of the wicked,
from the plots of evildoers.
They sharpen their tongues like swords
and aim cruel words like deadly arrows.
They shoot from ambush at the innocent;
they shoot suddenly, without fear.
They encourage each other in evil plans,
they talk about hiding their snares;
they say, "Who will see it?"
They plot injustice and say,
"We have devised a perfect plan!"
Surely the human mind and heart are cunning.
But God will shoot them with his arrows;
they will suddenly be struck down.
He will turn their own tongues against them
and bring them to ruin;
all who see them will shake their heads in scorn.

— TEN —

AHITHOPHEL
TO WHOM DO YOU LISTEN?

The Background

The story of Ahithophel is told in 2 Samuel 15–17. He is also mentioned in 2 Samuel 23:34; 1 Chronicles 27:33-34.

The Story

Ahithophel is David's legendary adviser, the most esteemed counselor in all Israel. A native of Giloh, Ahithophel's wisdom is proverbial. Both David and Absalom have great confidence in him, regarding his advice as "like that of one who inquires of God" (2 Samuel 16:23). There is cause for great distress on David's part when Ahithophel joins Absalom's conspiracy.

The rebellion Absalom leads develops almost imperceptibly. With great patience and intentionality, Absalom plans, promotes, and patronizes. After four years of careful preparation, Absalom is ready to launch the revolt from Hebron. The conspiracy gains credibility and momentum when Ahithophel joins Absalom.

As soon as David hears the news that Absalom has initiated a coup, he and his entire household flee Jerusalem, with the exception of ten concubines left to care for the palace. David recognizes the tactical advantage Absalom has gained by obtaining the counsel of Ahithophel. The news prompts David to offer a prayer that Ahithophel's advice will not be the asset to Absalom that it has been to David. David prays specifically, "LORD, turn Ahithophel's counsel into foolishness" (2 Samuel 15:31).

While David hastens to put distance between himself and Absalom, Hushai the Arkite is given the mission of establishing David's intelligence network by being an agent of espionage. He is to return to Jerusalem under the pretense of joining Absalom and the revolt, in hopes of gaining Absalom's trust and confidence and the opportunity to thwart the advice of Ahithophel. Hushai is successful in being accepted into Absalom's war council.

As Absalom enters Jerusalem, Ahithophel advises him to publicly violate David's royal harem, the members of which have been left behind to watch the palace. This will send an unmistakable message as to Absalom's intentions and will strengthen the resolve of those aligned with him. A tent is pitched on the roof of the palace—so all Israel will have no doubt about what is happening—and Absalom proceeds to follow Ahithophel's advice, thus fulfilling one of the grim terms of Nathan's pronouncement in 2 Samuel 12:11-12, "This is what the LORD says: 'Out of your own household I am going to bring calamity on you. Before your very eyes I will take your wives and give them to one who is close to you, and he will sleep with your wives in broad daylight. You did it in secret, but I will do this thing in broad daylight before all Israel.'"

Absalom consults both Ahithophel and Hushai, asking each to give advice as to his next steps. Ahithophel encourages Absalom to authorize an immediate pursuit of David with twelve thousand men, taking full advantage of the exhausted, demoralized, and vulnerable state of David and his force. Ahithophel volunteers to lead the force himself, suggesting that he will destroy only David in a quick, surgical strike, and will bring all of David's troops safely back to Jerusalem, where Absalom can win them over. Absalom and his senior leaders think Ahithophel's suggestion is an excellent strategy.

Absalom then has Hushai summoned to see if he will corroborate Ahithophel's advice or give different counsel. In the interest of David, Hushai advises the opposite of Ahithophel, encouraging Absalom to gather a large, overwhelming force to destroy both David and his men. Hushai counsels Absalom to take the time necessary to muster all Israel against such a mighty man of war, lest the experienced and wily David devise a strategy that will defeat Absalom's limited forces and turn the momentum back toward David. Hushai's bid to buy David more time is successful, perhaps because Hushai appeals to Absalom's ego by suggesting that Absalom himself lead the huge fighting force into battle and ensure his fame with a glorious, total conquest.

When Absalom chooses the advice of Hushai over Ahithophel, David's prayer is answered. The good advice of Ahithophel is frustrated, and the consequences prove disastrous for Absalom.

That is the end of Ahithophel's advice. It is also the end of Ahithophel. He realizes that the cause of Absalom is now lost, and the record of what then transpires is both poignant and tragic. After seeing his counsel rejected for what is perhaps the first time in his life—and what is certainly the last time—Ahithophel's response is to return to Giloh and take his own life. His sad ending is recorded in 2 Samuel 17:23: "When Ahithophel saw that his advice had not been followed, he saddled his donkey and set out for his house in his hometown. He put his house in order and then hanged himself. So he died and was buried in his father's tomb."

Hushai delivers the results of Absalom's council of war to the priests Zadok and Abiathar, who in turn dispatch their sons, Jonathan and Ahimaaz, to deliver the message to David. The sons of the two priests successfully inform David of Absalom's intentions, despite narrowly escaping capture by Absalom's forces.

Leadership Lessons

1. The unfaithfulness of leaders often results in the disloyalty of followers.

It is difficult to understand why an esteemed royal adviser like Ahithophel would turn traitor. A deeper study of the story, however, reveals Ahithophel's possible provocation. The first clue is found in the passage that describes David's sin with Bathsheba. When David inquires as to her identity, the word comes back, "She is Bathsheba, the daughter of Eliam and the wife of Uriah the Hittite" (2 Samuel 11:3). The second clue is found in 2 Samuel 23:24-39, where we find a list of David's great men of valor—the Thirty. Both Uriah and Eliam are mentioned among these highly decorated and honored military heroes. We also learn something else here. Eliam's father is Ahithophel of Giloh. This means Bathsheba is Ahithophel's granddaughter. These details lead us to the logical conclusion that David's sin with Bathsheba is likely the root of Ahithophel's eventual change of heart toward David.

One can easily imagine that Ahithophel develops a certain bitterness toward David, the murderer of his grandson-in-law and the corrupter of his granddaughter. Perhaps Ahithophel carries that grudge for years until he finally has the opportunity to abandon David and join Absalom's rebellion.

The disloyalty and unfaithfulness of a leader can result in the defection of key followers. David later writes, "Even my close friend, someone I trusted, one who shared my bread, has turned against me" (Psalm 41:9).

Relationships are critical to leadership, and trust and faithfulness are critical to relationships. David's sin with Bathsheba is probably what devastates his relationship with his most valuable adviser, adding to the price David ultimately pays for his sin.

The loyalty of followers is often dependent upon the faithfulness of leaders.

2. The ability to discern whose advice to follow is critical to a leader's success.

Every leader needs trusted advisers to give counsel and help explore options. Such wise individuals can provide valuable information and insights.

Reminiscent of Robert E. Lee's desirability to both the North and the South in the U.S. Civil War, both David and Absalom recognize the value of Ahithophel's counsel and want his valuable contribution for their own purposes. Ahithophel chooses Absalom's side, but Absalom chooses Hushai's counsel—the counsel that most appeals to his vanity and pride and promises to make him look the best.

When everyone on your team is giving you the same advice, the decision is usually easy to make. When there are dissenting views, the ability to discern whose advice is best becomes necessary. The elements of that discernment can include the track record of the adviser, the probability of success, the leader's confidence in the adviser, and a consideration of risk versus reward.

One pitfall of leadership is making decisions based on the best interests of the leader, rather than making decisions based on the best interests of the organization, institution, or nation. This pitfall is often seen when leaders choose short-term, personal benefits over long-term, organizational benefits.[1] Any time a leader makes a decision based on personal benefit, the odds of long-term organizational success plummet.

Questions for Leadership Development

1. What role do trusted advisers play in your leadership?

2. Who are your trusted advisers, and what has given them that right in your life?

3. How could your trusted advisers lose the influence you have given them?

4. For whom are *you* a trusted adviser?

5. How does the faithfulness of leaders inspire loyalty in follow-ers?

6. What other leadership lessons can be derived from the story of Ahithophel?

The Psalm

Psalm 55 is reminiscent of the time Ahithophel joins with Absalom. When David hears of Ahithophel's betrayal, he prays, "LORD, turn Ahithophel's counsel into foolishness" (2 Samuel 15:31). That prayer is detailed further in Psalm 55.

Psalm 55:9-14

Lord, confuse the wicked, confound their words,
for I see violence and strife in the city.
Day and night they prowl about on its walls;
malice and abuse are within it.
Destructive forces are at work in the city;
threats and lies never leave its streets.
If an enemy were insulting me,
I could endure it;
if a foe were rising against me,
I could hide.
But it is you, a man like myself,
my companion, my close friend,
with whom I once enjoyed sweet fellowship
at the house of God,
as we walked about
among the worshipers.

— ELEVEN —

HUSHAI
EVEN A KING NEEDS A FRIEND

The Background

The story of Hushai is told in 2 Samuel 15–17; 1 Chronicles 27:33. He is also mentioned in 1 Kings 4:16.

The Story

As David is fleeing Absalom, his friend Hushai the Arkite catches up with him near the summit of the Mount of Olives. A weeping David leads what must look like a hurried funeral procession. With bare feet and a covered head—traditional signs of mourning—he is leaving Jerusalem in disgrace and dishonor. The City of David has become the city of Absalom—at least for a season.

Hushai appears immediately after David asks God to thwart the counsel of Ahithophel. It is as though he is the answer to David's prayer. With torn clothes and a dusty head, Hushai also shows visible signs of grief, in solidarity with his king. Hushai intends to accompany David, but the king has another idea. Hushai is told that he will be a burden if he accompanies David in the flight. Instead, he can best serve David by returning to Jerusalem, persuading Absalom to take him into his confidence, and working to frustrate the advice of Ahithophel. Hushai is to become a spy and keep David informed of what is happening at the highest levels of Absalom's rebellion. Any information Hushai gains can be relayed to Zadok and Abiathar, who will then relay the information to David via their sons, Ahimaaz and Jonathan. David now has five men strategically placed in Jerusalem. Abiathar, Zadok, Jonathan, Ahimaaz, and Hushai form his network of undercover intelligence agents.

Hushai hurries back to Jerusalem and arrives as Absalom and his supporters are entering the city. Seeking to establish his credibility, Hushai greets Absalom warmly, "Long live the king! Long live the king!" (2 Samuel 16:16). When Absalom asks Hushai why he would turn on his friend, David, and not accompany him into exile, Hushai indicates that he will give his allegiance to "the one chosen by the LORD, by these people, and by all the men of Israel" (2 Samuel 16:18), and further indicates that he will serve Absalom just as he has served David. Hushai's greeting and response to Absalom's question could apply either to David *or* to Absalom, but Hushai is deemed sincere and is welcomed into Absalom's inner circle of counselors.

Absalom then asks Ahithophel for advice. Ahithophel counsels Absalom to sleep with David's concubines, in plain sight of all Israel, so no one will miss the act or its significance. The deed will leave no doubt in the people's mind that David is no longer in charge, and will strengthen the resolve of Absalom's followers.

Ahithophel further counsels for an immediate, surgical, military strike that will take out only David, leaving the opportunity for Absalom to make peace with David's followers and allow them to transfer their loyalty to the new king. Ahithophel volunteers to lead the mission himself, while Absalom stays safely in Jerusalem. Absalom and his war council consider the advice to be sound and sage.

But in a strange twist, Absalom then asks Hushai if he concurs with Ahithophel's advice. With grand and elegant rhetoric, Hushai gives the speech of his life. He counters Ahithophel's advice by inferring that the plan underestimates David. Hushai reminds Absalom of David's ferocity and cunning, likening David in 2 Samuel 17:8 to "a wild bear robbed of her cubs"—with savvy and seasoned warriors who will be elusive and fierce, and who are capable of taking the initiative and successfully ambushing Absalom's troops. Such a defeat will throw Absalom's followers into a panic.

Hushai advises Absalom to take the time to gather troops from each of the twelve tribes, amassing a superior force "as numerous as the sand on the seashore" (2 Samuel 17:11). He promises that Absalom's forces will annihilate David's forces as they "fall on him as dew settles on the ground" (2 Samuel 17:12), even to the point of leveling any city that offers refuge to David and "drag it down into the valley until not so much as a pebble is left" (2 Samuel 17:13). Hushai appeals to Absalom's ego by suggesting that Absalom himself lead the troops in an overwhelming victory, destroying both David and those faithful to him.

Absalom finds Hushai's image of a grand and glorious victory to be much more appealing than Ahithophel's strategy. Hushai's advice, of course, is intended to benefit David, not Absalom. His counsel is designed to buy David time to refresh and regroup and prepare for the battle to come. The advice will also make Absalom vulnerable by personally involving him in the battle.

Hushai then gives a status report to David's agents—the priests Zadok and Abiathar—who have their sons, Jonathan and Ahimaaz, hasten to reach David with the urgent intelligence. When David receives the message, he and all those with him immediately cross the Jordan under cover of night to the safety of Mahanaim. Just as Hushai hoped, Absalom's delay in pursuing David allows the king the time he needs to strengthen and supply his army.

Leadership Lessons

1. There is a difference between a counselor and a confidant.

The difference between Hushai's relationship to David and Ahithophel's relationship to David is described in 1 Chronicles

27:33: "Ahithophel was the king's counselor. Hushai the Arkite was the king's confidant." There is a difference between an esteemed consultant and a trustworthy friend, and that is the difference between Ahithophel and Hushai.

Ahithophel is David's counselor, not in the capacity of a clinical therapist but in the capacity of a wide-ranging adviser. Such a counselor can be extremely valuable to a leader. Counselors can make helpful observations, present useful options, offer valuable suggestions, and provide beneficial data. A counselor can be hired. Not so with a confidant.

Hushai is David's confidant. A confidant is a faithful friend you trust with the intimate details of your life. A confidant is someone with whom your defenses can be lowered and you can be yourself. A confidant may not have the ability to produce the list of possibilities a counselor can generate, but a confidant has the ability to help you process those possibilities with your best interests in mind. A confidant can make helpful suggestions because a confidant knows you well.

King David needs both a counselor like Ahithophel and a confidant like Hushai. Leaders are wise to have both counselors and confidants.

2. When it comes to strategy, simple is often preferred over complicated.

Ahithophel's advice is simple, strategic, and unsophisticated: *Strike David. Strike hard. Strike now.* Hushai's advice, on the other hand, is complicated and elaborate and involves a significant amount of time, men, and planning.

The advice that is simple and direct is usually to be preferred over the advice that is ornate and extravagant. Hushai goes to great rhetorical lengths to persuade Absalom not to pursue David right away. His advice is full of hyperbole, contains the most impressive oratory, and strokes Absalom's ego.[1]

The best rhetoric does not necessarily mean the best counsel. Simple plans are often more effective than grand strategies.

3. There is nothing like a crisis to help leaders clearly identify their friends and enemies.

David's situation is perilous and desperate. No longer is he a king with the ability to lavish gifts upon friends and share perks with colleagues. David is running for his life. He and all those associated with him are in peril. In times like this, only those who are true friends stay by a leader's side. When others run *from* you, true friends run *to* you.

Although Scripture does not have a great deal to say about him, Hushai proves his friendship in a time of severe trial. When Absalom usurps David's reign of Israel, a crisis of epic proportions ensues for David. Hushai is there for his friend. At David's time of deepest need, his friend shows up, willing and able to help.

4. God's ultimate plan will not be thwarted.

Why does Absalom embrace the fantasy-based advice of Hushai and reject the clear-thinking counsel of Ahithophel? In the middle of the account of Absalom's revolt is a key verse that offers this theological explanation: "For the LORD had ordained to thwart the good counsel of Ahithophel, so that the LORD might bring calamity on Absalom" (2 Samuel 17:14, NASB).

The defeat of Absalom is brought about, not primarily by the strategy of David, not primarily by the clever deception of Hushai, not primarily by the foolishness of Absalom himself. The defeat of Absalom is brought about primarily by the providence and will of God. Such are the hidden, powerful purposes of God.

While Absalom is free to make his own decision regarding to whom he will listen and whose counsel he will accept, there is the sense that God—in ways not easily discerned at first—ensures that his divine plan is ultimately realized.

Questions for Leadership Development

1. Who are the counselors and confidants who make your leadership more effective?

2. Who has been a Hushai to you, and how can you best express your gratitude?

3. How can you be a Hushai to someone in need?

4. What other leadership lessons can be derived from the story of Hushai?

The Psalm

In the spirit of a lament, Psalm 140 contains David's prayer for divine protection and rescue from violent and treacherous foes. Suggestive of David's flight from Absalom and prayer that Ahithophel's counsel will be foiled, the psalmist remains trusting as he requests that the designs of the wicked not succeed. The psalm ends with a serene statement of praise and certain trust in the providence of God.

Psalm 140:1-8

Rescue me, LORD, from evildoers;
protect me from the violent,
who devise evil plans in their hearts
and stir up war every day.
They make their tongues as sharp as a serpent's;
the poison of vipers is on their lips.
Keep me safe, LORD, from the hands of the wicked;
protect me from the violent,
who devise ways to trip my feet.
The arrogant have hidden a snare for me;
they have spread out the cords of their net
and have set traps for me along my path.
I say to the LORD, "You are my God."
Hear, LORD, my cry for mercy.
Sovereign LORD, my strong deliverer,
you shield my head in the day of battle.
Do not grant the wicked their desires, LORD;
do not let their plans succeed.

TWELVE

ITTAI THE GITTITE
WHO'S BY YOUR SIDE?

The Background

The story of Ittai is told in 2 Samuel 15:18-22; 18:2-12.

The Story

When Absalom's rebellion becomes public, David and his followers escape Jerusalem in haste. The last house on the way out of the city becomes a temporary reviewing stand for David as his entourage flees the capital. From this vantage point, David is able to watch his followers march past and assess their number and condition. His officials and their families hurry by with whatever belongings they have been able to gather quickly and carry.

The Kerethites and Pelethites also accompany David. They are professional soldiers, distinct from Israel's regular army, elite troops who continue to serve David and provide his personal security.

Also in the procession escaping Jerusalem are six hundred Gittites who remain loyal to David. These foreign troops and their families are from Gath, the Philistine hometown of Goliath. While David was there in exile, some residents of the city became his committed followers. As the Gittites march past, David is surprised to see Ittai in their number. Ittai, "a bright spot in this dark story,"[1] is the first supporter of David to be identified by name during Absalom's revolt.

David singles out Ittai, unwilling to let the newcomer's loyalty go unnoticed. Since Ittai is not an Israelite and arrived "only yesterday" (2 Samuel 15:20), it seems unreasonable to David that Ittai risk his life and family by getting involved in David's dispute. Instead, David blesses him—"May the LORD show you faithfulness and kindness" (2 Samuel 15:20)—and encourages him to return to Jerusalem and "King" Absalom (2 Samuel 15:19). David offers Ittai an honorable way out, granting him a full pardon and releasing him from his commitment.

In response, Ittai delivers a moving statement of devotion to David: "As surely as the LORD lives, and as my lord the king lives, wherever my lord the king may be, whether it means life or death, there will your servant be" (2 Samuel 15:21).

Ittai knows that the decision to stay with David is also a decision to fight—and, potentially, to see his whole group destroyed. His offer includes more than just words of encouragement; it includes a willingness to share the danger.

One wonders if Ittai is aware of the story of David's great-grandmother, Ruth.[2] His oath of loyalty is reminiscent of Ruth's classic expression of devotion to Naomi: "Don't urge me to leave you or to turn back from you. Where you go I will go, and where you stay I will stay. Your people will be my people and your God my God. Where you die I will die, and there I will be buried. May the LORD deal with me, be it ever so severely, if even death separates you and me" (Ruth 1:16-17).

Perhaps Ittai knows the story of Ruth and carefully chooses his words to reflect her great statement of devotion. Or, perhaps Ittai is unaware of the story, but because his own character is so similar to Ruth's character, the words he uses are akin to hers. Either way, the impact and import of those words are not lost on David. The similarities between Ruth and Ittai are significant. Both are foreigners to Israel. Both express their commitment and devotion in ways that have, for centuries, been held up as examples of fidelity. Naomi and David, both Israelites, are the recipients of gracious and steadfast commitments that bless generations to come.

David then invites Ittai to march with him, which he does, with his troops and their families.

Once David and his followers reach the safety and security of Mahanaim, David divides his troops into three divisions—a third under the command of Joab, a third under the command of Joab's brother Abishai, and a third under Ittai. With the defeat of the rebellion and the death of Absalom, Ittai fades out of the biblical record and passes from view.

Leadership Lessons

1. "A real friend is one who walks in when others walk out."[3]

This has to have been one of the worst days of David's life. Many who have been followers become traitors. His own son is attempting to take not only his throne but also his life.

When David is at his point of greatest need, Ittai stands beside him. This is a true friend. Even after David urges him to depart for his own safety, Ittai says, "Wherever you go, I will go." That is a real friend. Ittai chooses to stand with David even when David's own son stands against him. He pledges allegiance to David with no assurance of benefit, only the promise of hardship.

It is said of Job, "Your words have supported those who stumbled; you have strengthened faltering knees" (Job 4:4). Perhaps the same can be said of Ittai. It may very well be that his words of encouragement cause David to stand when he might have stumbled. Though the circumstances are grim, Ittai's loyalty brightens David's day and lifts David's spirits.

When the chips are down and many people have turned away from you, if there is someone who is willing to stand by you, to give you a call, to tell you they have not forgotten you or forsaken you—that person is a blessing. And if that person is willing to share the danger you are in, that person is a gift from God.

2. It is possible for your enemy to become your ally.

A Gittite is a person from Gath. Gath is the hometown of Goliath, and a stronghold in a nation that is one of Israel's oldest enemies. The Philistines are bitter and hated foes of Israel.

Nevertheless, the elite palace guard is composed of Philistine warriors—Gittites—who became David's followers when he resided in Gath. That they are more than mercenaries is suggested by Ittai's expression of loyalty.

Sometimes the person who stands beside you today is someone who stood against you yesterday. David, whose rise to the throne is assured when he slays a Gittite named Goliath, will see that kingship preserved by the services of another Gittite named Ittai.

It is possible for enemies to become allies.

3. The reward for great loyalty is great trust.

It is ironic that David is fleeing Absalom, a son who has betrayed him, while at the same time being followed by Ittai, a foreigner who has befriended him. Although a stranger and not of Israel, Ittai is more faithful than many who are Israelites by birth. This inhabitant of Gath is determined to support David in all his trials. How admirable is the affirmation of his loyalty. His fidelity leads to a position of great trust.

Once David and his followers reach Mahanaim, David divides his troops into thirds, in preparation for the battle with Absalom's forces. A third of the troops are placed under the command of Joab, who has proven himself in battle time and time again and is David's top general. A third of the troops are placed under the command of Abishai, a warrior whose ability, loyalty, and faithfulness are unquestioned. And a third of the troops are placed under the command of Ittai the Gittite, whose loyalty has led David to entrust him with significant authority and responsibility.

The fruit of loyalty is trust.

Questions for Leadership Development

1. Under what circumstances can enemies become allies?

2. When the chips are down, who stands beside you?

3. To whom are you loyal, and how is that loyalty expressed?

4. What other leadership lessons can be derived from the story of Ittai?

The Psalm

The circumstances and life events from which Psalm 61 arose may very well have been David's flight from Absalom.

Psalm 61:1-4

Hear my cry, O God;
listen to my prayer.
From the ends of the earth I call to you,
I call as my heart grows faint;
lead me to the rock that is higher than I.
For you have been my refuge,
a strong tower against the foe.
I long to dwell in your tent forever
and take refuge in the shelter of your wings.

— THIRTEEN —

SHIMEI
THE EXHAUSTING EFFECT OF CRITICISM

The Background

The story of Shimei is told in 2 Samuel 16:5-14; 19:15-23; 1 Kings 2:8-9, 36-46.

The Story

Shimei is a common name in ancient Israel—at least a dozen different individuals bear that name in the Old Testament.[1] The best-known of them—and the particular Shimei we are interested in—lives near Bahurim and is the son of Gera. This Shimei is from the same tribe as Saul, which may help explain why he holds such a deep grudge against King David, of the tribe of Judah.

We first meet Shimei on one of the darkest days in King David's life, when David and his entourage are forced to flee Jerusalem during the attempted coup by his own son Absalom. David is barely out of the capital city when he encounters Shimei at a village on the eastern slope of the Mount of Olives. Adding to the humiliation of the hasty retreat are the brash actions and bitter accusations of Shimei, who antagonizes the hard-pressed king as he passes through Bahurim. Thinking that David's days as ruler are over, Shimei vents his rage at David with words and actions designed to further discredit the king.

Apparently David's flight to the Jordan leads through a narrow ravine, and Shimei runs along a parallel ridge, hurling curses, stones, and dirt at David and his men. As the king's party hurries along the road, Shimei jeers at them, following their progress from his vantage point while dishing both verbal and physical dirt at King David. David, fleeing for his life, is being assaulted by a man acting like a deranged lunatic.

From a rival tribe with political grounds for hostility, Shimei is playing a very dangerous game. He is passionate and bitter, and his words go beyond criticism to insults.[2] He desires to disgrace David as an unlawful usurper of Saul's throne. Shimei shows his contempt by calling the king a murderer and a scoundrel, interpreting Absalom's rebellion as divine punishment for David's acts against Saul, and broadcasting that David is getting exactly what he has coming.

The warriors who accompany David are shocked at Shimei's fearless abuse of the king, and their first impulse is to permanently silence Shimei. Abishai, one of David's protective detail, calls Shimei a "dead dog" (2 Samuel 16:9) whose insults are not to be tolerated, and asks for permission to cut off Shimei's head. David, however, humbly submits himself to the ranting lunatic. In a moment of marked restraint, the king counsels mercy, wondering aloud if God himself might be behind Shimei's actions. "My son, my own flesh and blood, is trying to kill me. How much more, then, this Benjamite! Leave him alone; let him curse, for the LORD has told him to" (2 Samuel 16:11). The experience exhausts David and his men, and they find themselves completely drained by the time they reach Mahanaim.

The next meeting of David and Shimei is very different. As David returns to Jerusalem after Absalom's rebellion has been put down, the men of David's tribe of Judah meet him at Gilgal to help him cross the Jordan. With the men of Judah, incredibly, is the Benjamite Shimei. He has scurried to the Jordan as though his life depends upon him arriving in time—which may well be the case. Shimei, eager to make amends for his treasonous words and subversive actions, brings with him a thousand other Benjamites to pledge allegiance to King David.

Shimei's actions at this point are exactly opposite to what happened as David left Jerusalem. No longer cursing David with bold braggadocio, Shimei assumes the position of a humble penitent. He falls to the ground before the king and begs for his life, seeking forgiveness for his prior disrespect, and vowing his allegiance. Again, Abishai suggests that it would be appropriate to cut off Shimei's head. And, again, David mercifully spares Shimei with a royal reprieve, refusing to mar the joy of his triumphant return with a show of vengeance on his enemies.

The record of Shimei picks up again many years later, when David is old and is transferring the throne to his son Solomon. David, in his dying charge to Solomon, instructs Solomon to finally avenge Shimei's prior insult: "Bring his gray head down to the grave in blood" (1 Kings 2:9).

Unlike his father, Solomon is no warrior; but, like David, Solomon is also no fool when it comes to political reality. Solomon does not proceed to act quickly on his father's instructions but instead restricts Shimei to the confines of Jerusalem.[3] Solomon calls for Shimei and, in effect, puts him under modified house arrest, instructing him to stay in Jerusalem with the understanding that if he ever leaves the city, he will be executed.[4] Solomon's wisdom is evidenced in this edict. By restricting Shimei to Jerusalem, Solomon can execute him for a different transgression than that for which his father, David, granted pardon.

Three years later, when two of Shimei's servants run away, Shimei follows them to Gath and brings them home. When Solomon learns that Shimei has broken parole, Benaiah is granted the command that Abishai twice longed to hear many years before, and Shimei's gray head is placed in the grave. With that act, "the kingdom was now established in Solomon's hands" (1 Kings 2:46).

Leadership Lessons

1. When facing criticism, keep moving.

It is important to note that David does not let Shimei and his unwarranted criticism stop him in his tracks. He and his entourage continue moving toward their destination.

This certainly is not the first time David faces criticism. Before David faces Goliath, he faces the criticism of his brother Eliab, who disparages David for even considering battling the giant. David does not then let his brother's criticism stop him from pursuing the task at hand, nor does he later let Shimei's criticism deter him from his objective.

Criticism can have a paralyzing effect. Leaders are often tempted to let destructive criticism stop them in their tracks while they deal with those who are dishing the dirt. Do not let criticism bring the mission to a grinding halt. Do not let criticism stop your forward progress.

While a lot of criticism *is* unwarranted and falls into the persecution category, some criticism can be valuable. Constructive criticism often contains truth and reveals needed adjustments. Do not miss opportunities to make those adjustments when necessary. Ask yourself, *Is there a kernel of truth in this criticism? Is there something God wants to speak into my life through this person? Does this criticism shed light on an area I need to examine?*

2. When facing criticism, respond with grace and humility.

Shimei represents all those whose criticism of leadership is full of bitter impudence. It is one thing for a leader to accept criticism when offered courteously. It is quite another thing not to react when attacked publicly in an unkind manner, let alone when the criticism is accompanied by curses and violence. Shimei is the kind of person who kicks you when you are down. Yet David shows amazing self-control, proving that he is a leader who is able to overlook the kinds of hurtful comments all leaders endure at one time or another.

The ability to handle criticism well is a gift that can be developed, perhaps by giving attention to the example of self-control David provides when facing Shimei's criticism. There are some valuable lessons to be learned here: When criticism is given harshly, do not respond in kind. Develop a thick skin and a tender heart. The temptation is to develop a thin, hypersensitive skin and a tough, hypercritical heart. Seek to identify the root of the criticism. David demonstrates the art of empathy, acknowledging that, as a Benjamite, Shimei may have good reason to feel the way he does. Acknowledge your own shortcomings. David is well aware of his own failures.[5]

The power to dispense mercy is a prerogative of authority.[6] David is merciful to Shimei at their first meeting and magnanimous at their second. David has dodged spears before. Now he has dodged sticks and stones, as well as words. It is a gracious leader who can sidestep spears, rocks, words, and memories.

All leaders eventually learn that people who are hurt say hurtful things. Receiving those hurtful words is part of the price of leadership. When facing criticism, respond graciously.

3. When facing criticism, find ways to refresh yourself.

Criticism can have an exhausting effect. By the time David and his men reach the Jordan River, they are exhausted. It is not just the journey that wearies them. It is also the criticism they have faced along the way. Dealing with criticism can be emotionally draining and physically taxing. As was the case in this situation with David, criticism often comes our way when we are already under stress.

Facing criticism is an inherent part of leadership. No matter how much we dislike being criticized, we can count on criticism accompanying the work we have been given, which means we need to learn to deal with it effectively.

There, by the Jordan, David "refreshed himself" (2 Samuel 16:14). Perhaps it is the presence of the water itself that is so helpful to David. Early in my ministry, while pastoring along the Ohio River, I discovered the therapeutic qualities of water. Lunch at a favorite restaurant overlooking the Ohio River almost always improved my outlook and attitude. Water can have both a calming and invigorating effect. Water refreshes. Spending time near and in water can be restorative.

Perhaps it is the relationship of water to sacrament that gives it this potential for therapeutic invigoration. There at the Jordan David finds a place where he can drown the criticism he has endured, and give it a proper death, rather than carry it any farther on his already difficult journey.[7]

Leaders must find ways to refresh themselves during seasons when they experience significant and exhausting criticism.

4. When giving criticism, remember that words have consequences.

Much to his chagrin, Shimei's words have shelf life. Once spoken, words cannot be unspoken. Each of us is capable of voicing both blessings and curses. Words matter. And so do the people who hear them.

There are many Bible verses that tell us to be careful with our words. Here are just a couple of examples:

"A gentle answer turns away wrath, but a harsh word stirs up anger" (Proverbs 15:1).

"Those who guard their mouths and their tongues keep themselves from calamity" (Proverbs 21:23).

Those who follow Shimei's example of freely spewing bitter criticism may also suffer from "Dead Dog Syndrome," which results in the loss of one's head. Shimei may have figuratively lost his head that day at Bahurim, and as a result, the day comes when he literally loses his head in Jerusalem.

In our day and age, criticism is not just experienced verbally and in person. The internet, and especially social media, have made criticism a virtual sport. Today's critics often throw cyber dirt and rocks, and wise leaders will model for their followers the grace-filled response of David, rather than responding in kind.

If you hold a grudge, your bitterness may come out at a most inopportune time and result in your losing your head! When giving criticism, one is wise to keep that in mind.

Questions for Leadership Development

1. How do you respond when, like David, you are harshly criticized?

2. What are some healthy ways a leader can respond to criticism?

3. How do you respond when, like Shimei, you are the one harshly criticizing, and it becomes apparent that you are in error?

4. What other leadership lessons can be derived from the story of Shimei?

The Psalm

So many of the words, phrases, and milieu of Psalm 22 reflect the travail of a leader experiencing criticism, as David experiences in his interaction with Shimei.

Psalm 22:6-11

But I am a worm and not a man,
scorned by everyone, despised by the people.
All who see me mock me;
they hurl insults, shaking their heads.
"He trusts in the Lord," they say,
"let the Lord rescue him.
Let him deliver him,
since he delights in him."
Yet you brought me out of the womb;
you made me trust in you, even at my mother's breast.
From birth I was cast on you;
from my mother's womb you have been my God.
Do not be far from me,
for trouble is near
and there is no one to help.

— FOURTEEN —

BARZILLAI
THE IMPORTANCE OF SUPPLY LINES

The Background

The story of Barzillai is told in 2 Samuel 17:27-29; 19:31-39; 1 Kings 2:7. He is also mentioned in Ezra 2:61; Nehemiah 7:63.

The Story

When David learns of Absalom's rebellion, he wastes no time in fleeing Jerusalem. As Absalom is entering the city through one gate, David is leaving the city by way of another. When you are trying to escape with your life, little thought is given to such luxuries as taking a change of clothes or packing a lunch. David is traveling light. Speed is of the essence.

By the time David and his followers reach Mahanaim, they are physically exhausted from the rigors of the journey and emotionally exhausted from enduring Shimei's criticism, curses, and clods. Mahanaim has rich historical significance, dating back to the time of Jacob.[1] The first mention of Mahanaim is in Genesis 32:2. There, Jacob has a vision of angels and—alarmed at the approach of his brother, whom he has good reason to fear—divides his entourage into two companies. David, perhaps reminded of Jacob's anxiety and strategy, and moved by a similar anxiety at the approach of his son, divides his troops into three companies against Absalom.

At Mahanaim David is met by three men: Shobi, son of Nahash from Rebbah of the Ammonites; Makir, son of Ammiel from Lo Debar; and Barzillai, the Gileadite from Rogelim. We do not know much about Shobi. This is the only time he is mentioned in the Bible. Makir is the kind of person who takes care of people when they are in need. Makir lives in Lo Debar and took in Mephibosheth, the disabled son of Jonathan, when Mephibosheth fled for his life after the death of his father and grandfather. Barzillai is the leader of these three men. A wealthy eighty-year-old from Gilead, Barzillai is acquainted with the lay of the land and is aware of what provisions will be essential to sustain David and his men.

Barzillai and his friends bring with them the kinds of practical supplies David needs—bedding, eating utensils, and food. These provisions are akin to manna from heaven for the exhausted, famished king and his entourage. A welcome expression of loyalty to David's beleaguered forces, the provisions buoy David, refresh his men, and provide supplies they will need to battle Absalom.

After Absalom's rebellion is crushed, David sets out on his return to Jerusalem. When he reaches the Jordan, David is greeted first by the groveling Shimei; then by Mephibosheth, who is burdened by a need to set the record straight and clear his name; and, finally, by the life-saving Barzillai, ready to once again escort David across the Jordan and give public expression of his continued support.

David wants to reward Barzillai for his services and invites him to accompany him to Jerusalem, where he will enjoy the pleasures of the palace as David's honored guest. Barzillai declines, citing his age as the major factor. He feels an octogenarian like himself will be a burden to David. Since his senses have become dulled with age (he can barely see beauty, taste delicacies, smell perfume, or hear music), he feels it would be a shame to waste the extravagance of the king's table on someone like himself, who cannot enjoy it to the fullest. Instead, he requests that the offer be extended to Kimham[2] in his place, which David gladly honors. Then David kisses Barzillai farewell, and Barzillai returns home.[3]

Years later, when David gives his final charge to Solomon, he instructs Solomon to look favorably on the sons of Barzillai, proving that David has never forgotten Barzillai's benevolence.[4]

Leadership Lessons

1. Do not underestimate the importance of supply lines.

All leaders are dependent on supply lines. It is seldom possible for leaders—military, corporate, or spiritual—to carry everything with them they will need for the duration of a specific mission. That is why supply lines are so critical. You can go without them for a brief season if you are well prepared, but you cannot go without them for very long.

Physical supply lines provide for important needs such as food, shelter, rest, and exercise. Emotional supply lines offer community, relationships, encouragement, and support networks. Financial supply lines make available resources for life and for mission. Spiritual supply lines provide means to build faith and experience grace.

In military strategy, supply lines are critical—the development, maintenance, and protection of supply lines is essential, as is the interruption or destruction of your enemy's supply lines. When your supply lines are lacking, most often what is compromised is your ability to achieve your mission. However, there are times when an absence of adequate supply lines results in the destruction of the resources around you. Either way, without supply lines, destruction results—either yours, or that of your surroundings.

This is most easily seen in the strategy of Major General William T. Sherman's march from Atlanta to Savannah, Georgia, in 1864. Sherman's strategy was to intentionally forgo supply lines and live off the land. His strategy was characterized as a "scorched earth" policy. Advancing Union troops were ordered to burn crops, kill livestock, consume supplies, and destroy railroads and manufacturing capabilities to keep goods from falling into Confederate hands. This tactic not only provided needed resources for Sherman's army; it also rendered the Confederate economy incapable of resupplying its soldiers, leading eventually, as we all know, to the defeat of the Confederacy.

When organizations and institutions fail to develop and maintain adequate supply lines, damage and destruction will be the result. Leaders should make a priority of giving sufficient attention to developing and maintaining adequate supply lines for their organizations and for themselves.

Too many organizations do not take the prudent step of insisting on having enough resources on hand to weather a financial storm. Like Joseph's preparations in Egypt, leaders are wise to prepare for sudden challenges, regardless of the type of organizations we lead. Barzillai has a storehouse from which to draw. So should we. The success of the mission is partially dependent on the success of the supply line.

2. A loyal friend is a priceless treasure.

Even though David has his detractors and his insurgents, he still has a circle of people who remain faithful to him. Here we learn the value of friendship and loyalty. Mahanaim is the name Jacob gave the place where angels came and ministered to him.[5]

When David desperately needs support at the time of Absalom's rebellion, Barzillai rallies to his side, bringing necessary provisions to the hungry, thirsty followers of David. Barzillai offers David unwavering loyalty and a hero's scorn of consequences. If Absalom prevails, it is likely Barzillai will suffer for his loyalty. As it turns out, David prevails, and Barzillai is rewarded for his loyalty.

Loyal friends are easily identified when times become bad. In times of intense struggle and critical need, you want friends who will come running to you, not friends who run from you. To gain a friend with characteristics like loyalty, courtesy, and hospitality, a leader needs to *be* a friend with characteristics like loyalty, courtesy, and hospitality. Now is the time to be cultivating both those friendships and those characteristics.

One of the reasons Barzillai, Shobi, and Makir are able to respond with loyalty is that David is still in the fight. In the midst of personal and professional disaster, although David is retreating, he is not surrendering. Leaders must keep hope alive long enough for help to arrive.[6]

3. Your children may be the ones who most benefit from your kindness to others.

Barzillai is a father who wants to pass along blessings to his children. As David is crossing the Jordan upon his return to Jerusalem, Barzillai suggests that his son Kimham be the beneficiary of David's generosity. It is important to recognize that, before Barzillai's children benefit from David's kindness, they have already benefited from their father's kindness.

Late in David's life, he gives his son Solomon instructions concerning Solomon's transition to the kingship. In that charge, David instructs Solomon to provide for Barzillai's children. Notably, Barzillai is the only individual David mentions in a positive light as being worthy of Solomon's special, gracious consideration.

Questions for Leadership Development

1. What is the condition of your personal supply lines? What is the condition of your organization's supply lines?

2. How can you strengthen your personal supply lines? How can you strengthen your organization's supply lines?

3. What friendships are you cultivating?

4. How can you be a supply line for someone else?

5. What other leadership lessons can be derived from the story of Barzillai?

The Psalm

We do not know when David wrote Psalm 23, the most familiar of the Psalms. It may very well have been when Absalom tried to become king. As David flees Jerusalem and makes his way to the Jordan River, he is certainly walking through the valley of the shadow of death. As he makes his way into Gilead, he meets Barzillai, who "prepared a table for him," offering provisions, safety, and rest.

Psalm 23

The LORD is my shepherd, I lack nothing.
He makes me lie down in green pastures,
he leads me beside quiet waters,
he refreshes my soul.
He guides me along the right paths
for his name's sake.
Even though I walk
through the darkest valley,
I will fear no evil,
for you are with me;
your rod and your staff,
they comfort me.
You prepare a table before me
in the presence of my enemies.
You anoint my head with oil;
my cup overflows.
Surely your goodness and love will follow me
all the days of my life,
and I will dwell in the house of the LORD
forever.

— FIFTEEN —

AHIMAAZ
GOOD MAN; GOOD NEWS

The Background

The story of Ahimaaz is told in 2 Samuel 15:23-29; 17:15-22; 18:19-29. He is also mentioned in 1 Kings 4:15; 1 Chronicles 6:8-9, 53.

The Story

Ahimaaz, a descendent of Aaron, is the son of Zadok the high priest. During Absalom's revolt, Ahimaaz proves his loyalty by becoming an agent for King David. As David flees from Absalom, Zadok and Abiathar and a host of Levites join him as he leaves Jerusalem, bringing with them the ark of the covenant. Ahimaaz is probably one of the priests who carries the ark that day. The priests offer sacrifices, imploring divine protection and favor upon David's followers as they leave the city. David then sends Zadok and Abiathar and their sons back to Jerusalem with his blessing. They are instructed to return the ark to Jerusalem, where they will serve as David's agents. Ahimaaz, Zadok's son, and Jonathan, Abiathar's son, are to relay vital information from Hushai the Arkite, David's confidant, back to David. Thus begins a saga filled with secret agents and subterfuge.

Hushai is able to convince Absalom to disregard the advice of Ahithophel and take the time to gather his forces, a tactic which provides David and his men valuable time to escape. Hushai then relays the vital intelligence to Zadok and Abiathar, who are to dispatch Ahimaaz and Jonathan at once with the news. The two high priests—Zadok and Abiathar—entrust the message to a servant girl, who carries it secretly to En Rogel, a spring located just to the east of Jerusalem, where Ahimaaz and Jonathan are waiting. The two young emissaries are positioned there because of the danger of being seen in Jerusalem. They are to relay the message to David and his men, notifying him to make haste to cross the Jordan, lest Absalom's men locate and overwhelm them.

Unfortunately, Ahimaaz and Jonathan are spotted by one of Absalom's followers, and troops are quickly dispatched to apprehend them. Fearing capture, the two flee En Rogel and reach Bahurim, the same village on the eastern slope of the Mount of Olives where Shimei cursed David as he fled Jerusalem. There they find a clever hiding place and conceal themselves in a well, located in the courtyard of a sympathizer's home. The homeowner's wife camouflages their hiding place by spreading out a cloth over the well and scattering wheat over it. When Absalom's patrol arrives, the woman sends the soldiers on a wild goose chase, telling them the two young men were last seen heading for the border. The soldiers search in that direction but, finding nothing, they return to Jerusalem.

After the patrol is gone, Ahimaaz and Jonathan climb out of the well and set off to inform David, who follows the advice of Hushai and crosses the Jordan with all haste. By daybreak David and his men are safe on the other side.

Ahimaaz next appears at the end of the battle between David's men and Absalom's men in the forest of Ephraim. Absalom has just been slain and his followers routed when Ahimaaz asks Joab for permission to run to David with the news of the victory. Joab denies the request, suggesting that David will not welcome the news of the death of his son, and Joab does not want Ahimaaz to be the bearer of what David will consider bad news. The implication is that Ahimaaz may be a recipient of David's wrath if he brings this message, and Joab wants to spare him the king's anger. However, Eugene Peterson proposes that Joab's motivation is actually self-protection: "Joab tells Ahimaaz that he doesn't want him to go because he wants to protect him from David's response to the news of Absalom's death. But the person he really wants to protect is himself."[1]

Instead, Joab dispatches a Cushite to run with the message of Absalom's death. The Cushite would be a native of Ethiopia or Nubia in southern Egypt, and is apparently serving as a mercenary in David's army. As a mercenary, it's plausible that the Cushite might be unaware of the personal details surrounding this particular battle—namely, that David specifically ordered his commanders at the outset of the battle not to harm Absalom. Therefore, he could be unaware of the fact that news of Absalom's death will bring the king sorrow. Bill Arnold suggests, "Joab simply wants someone he can rely on to report the outcome of the battle *and* the death of Absalom as good news. Ahimaaz is too intimate with the details to be objective and would not report the death of Absalom as good news, as Joab wants."[2] Perhaps Joab's motive here is still self-protection in that, if David presumes that a mercenary killed Absalom (rather than Joab), then Joab will remain safe from David's wrath.

After the Cushite has been sent, Ahimaaz asks a second time for permission to run. Joab reminds him that there will be no reward for the bearer of what David will perceive as bad news. But Ahimaaz does not give up easily. Joab finally relents and allows Ahimaaz to run but only after the Cushite has the advantage of an earlier start. Ahimaaz chooses to take a different route and, as a result, is the first to arrive at Mahanaim.[3]

David's watchman glimpses Ahimaaz in the distance. When the sentry announces that a runner is approaching, David anticipates good news.[4] Then the Cushite is spotted by the lookout. David continues to anticipate good news. As the first runner nears, the lookout announces that it appears to be Ahimaaz. David's estimation of Ahimaaz is reflected in his response: "He's a good man. He comes with good news" (2 Samuel 18:27).

Upon arriving, Ahimaaz announces victory. David has only one question: "Is the young man Absalom safe?" (2 Samuel 18:29). Ahimaaz, perhaps wishing to spare the feelings of the king, is able to sidestep the question, claiming that the victory has caused great confusion and commotion. The Cushite arrives about that time and is more than happy to blurt out the news of the death of Absalom. The report devastates David.

The biblical account of Ahimaaz ends with his significant run.

Leadership Lessons

1. In order to make good decisions, it is important to have good information.

As Absalom's revolt gains momentum, David knows that good information will be imperative if he is to make good decisions; indeed, if he is to survive. Hushai, Abiathar, Zadok, Ahimaaz, and Jonathan provide David with a network of spies who are key to the flow of valuable data and military intelligence.

To make good decisions, leaders need information that is both reliable and relevant. That information needs to be delivered in an opportune fashion in order to allow decisions to be made in a timely and prudent manner. This is why organizations invest significant resources in research and the gathering of data.

It is also important to note that even bad news can often provide good information. Bad news—if it is reliable and relevant—can prompt prudent responses that keep bad news from becoming worse news. Leaders should keep in mind that punishing the bearers of bad news will lead to communication barriers that often result in leaders not knowing that bad things are happening until it is too late to respond effectively.

Leaders have to actively pursue accurate information, and avoid behavior that makes people hesitant to provide accurate information—especially when it is bad news. Leaders who respond poorly to bad news often find themselves without the information they need.[6]

Accurate information, delivered in a timely manner, is imperative to leadership success.

2. Good people are often known for bringing good news.

Ahimaaz's delivery of the message of Absalom's defeat is not the first message Ahimaaz has delivered to David. He also delivered the message from Hushai that David should make haste crossing the Jordan in his flight from Absalom. Apparently there was something in the way Ahimaaz delivered that message that David appreciated. Thus, when he learns it is Ahimaaz approaching with news from the battle, David says, "He's a good man. He brings good news" (2 Samuel 18:27).

A good person brings good news, or at least delivers bad news in a good way. Some people have the ability to relay bad news in ways that reflect sensitivity and empathy. They are relationally gifted, mindful of the hearer's emotional condition, and careful to couch their communication in ways that cushion the impact of devastating news.

3. It sometimes makes sense to take a different route than others are taking.

The Cushite takes one route; Ahimaaz takes another.

A GPS often indicates more than one route option for a given destination. The shortest route is not always the fastest route. The most direct route may include difficult terrain, congestion, or other impediments that slow travel. The longer route can sometimes be faster.

Leaders should bear in mind that there is often more than one way to reach an objective, whether in transportation or logistics or systems. Given each particular situation, the choice of the best route may depend upon whether ease, speed, scenery, cost, or some other consideration should be the determining factor.

4. Motivation will often outdistance talent.

One can reasonably infer that Joab's choice of the Cushite runner is based on the Cushite's ability. It is easy to imagine that the Ethiopian (or Nubian) is a gifted runner. That area is still known for producing world-class distance runners. We know nothing of the Cushite's motivation, other than that his general has given him orders to run.

On the other hand, Ahimaaz's persistent pleas that he be permitted to run suggest significant motivation. As to the basis of his motivation, Ahimaaz may be seeking a reward, as Joab assumes. But it could be that Ahimaaz wants to get to David before the Cushite out of consideration for the king's feelings. Perhaps Ahimaaz seeks to prepare David for the news of his son's death by telling him the good news first. Or, maybe Ahimaaz thinks that the first news David hears should be from a friend. That will be better than having a stranger tell the bad news to David without any concern for or awareness of the personal impact the information will have on the king.

Whatever the *reason* of his motivation, the *result* of his motivation is that Ahimaaz outruns the Cushite.

Motivation often trumps giftedness. In many areas of life, the one who is most incentivized will often out-perform the one who is most gifted. However, the combination of motivation *and* giftedness almost always results in success.

Questions for Leadership Development

1. In what situations is it important that you be the first one to share the news?

2. What can a bearer of bad news do to ensure the news is communicated sensitively and to make the news more palatable?

3. What is your strategy for obtaining reliable and relevant, useful information?

4. What other leadership lessons can be derived from the story of Ahimaaz?

The Psalm

In Psalm 112, David extols the blessings for those who obey the commands of the Lord. He refers to the blessing of not fearing news, and the certain end of the wicked, which are reminiscent of the chapter of David's life in which Ahimaaz appears.

Psalm 112:6-10

Surely the righteous will never be shaken;
they will be remembered forever.
They will have no fear of bad news;
their hearts are steadfast, trusting in the LORD.
Their hearts are secure, they will have no fear;
in the end they will look in triumph on their foes.
They have freely scattered their gifts to the poor,
their righteousness endures forever;
their horn will be lifted high in honor.
The wicked will see and be vexed,
they will gnash their teeth and waste away;
the longings of the wicked will come to nothing.

— SIXTEEN —

SHEBA
OF AMBITION AND REBELLION

The Background

The story of Sheba, son of Bikri, is told in 2 Samuel 20:1-22.

The Story

As David returns to Jerusalem following the defeat of Absalom in the Forest of Ephraim, it becomes apparent that much work needs to be done to restore the unity of the kingdom. David only makes it as far as the Jordan River before tensions flare between the ten tribes of northern Israel and the tribe of Judah.

At the Jordan, all of Judah and half of Israel meet David to accompany him across the river. On the other side, an argument breaks out between those who have brought the king across the Jordan and those who wait on the other side. Those who wait accuse those who have brought David over of "stealing the king away" (2 Samuel 19:41). The men of Judah respond that, even though they are related to David, they have not taken advantage of that kinship in any way.

In the midst of the growing tension, a troublemaker named Sheba, son of Bikri, takes advantage of the intertribal rivalries and incites a rebellion. Like Saul, he is of the tribe of Benjamin. There, on the bank of the Jordan, a defiant Sheba plays on the jealousy that is aroused among the tribes of Israel by Judah's honor of being the first tribe to greet David at the Jordan. Sheba uses a trumpet to gain the attention of the tribes then proclaims that Israel will have nothing to do with David. "Every man to his tent!" (2 Samuel 20:1) is Sheba's rallying cry, reflecting a resistance steeped in deeply rooted tribal loyalties.[1]

Instead of escorting David to Jerusalem, the men of Israel desert the king and march to their homeland, following Sheba. However, the members of the tribe of Judah remain loyal to David and continue to accompany him from the Jordan to Jerusalem.

Having just survived Absalom's rebellion, David is not inclined to give a new rebellion time to gain momentum. The king is motivated to put the insurgency down quickly and decisively. As soon as David reaches Jerusalem, he appoints his nephew Amasa, a son of David's sister Abigail, as field commander for the battle to come. David commissions Amasa to muster the men of Judah, and gives him three days to accomplish it. After three days, when Amasa has not yet returned, David appoints another nephew, Abishai, a son of David's sister Zeruiah, to begin the pursuit of Sheba. Abishai is to take his brother Joab's men and pursue Sheba before Sheba is able to gain safety and security in a fortified city. The hunt is on.

Abishai marches out of Jerusalem with Joab's men, as well as the Kerethites and Pelethites and the mighty warriors. When they reach Gibeon, Amasa appears, on his way back to Jerusalem with the men he has belatedly mustered. There at Gibeon, Joab, who has accompanied Abishai, murders the unsuspecting Amasa by stabbing him in the belly.

Meanwhile, Sheba is gathering followers as he makes his way through all the tribes of Israel. Joab and Abishai and their troops march through Israel all the way to Abel Beth Maakah, the fortified city in which Sheba has taken refuge. Along the way, Joab apparently gains command of the forces David entrusted to Abishai, who perhaps became intimidated after seeing what Joab is capable of doing to any who contest his right to command.

When Joab and the troops arrive at Abel Beth Maakah, they build a siege ramp against the city and begin to batter the outer fortifications in order to bring the wall down. Joab intends to destroy the city and everyone in it.

While they are battering the fortifications, they are interrupted by the calls of a woman atop the wall. She asks for a parley with Joab, who goes forward to talk with her. The woman asks Joab why he is intent on destroying a peaceful and faithful city in Israel, adding, "Why do you want to swallow up the LORD's inheritance?" (2 Samuel 20:19).

Joab responds that he has no desire to destroy the city. His only aim is to stop the rebellion Sheba is leading against King David. "Hand over this one man, and I'll withdraw from the city" (2 Samuel 20:21). The woman responds that Sheba's head will be thrown over the wall to Joab. She shares her advice with the inhabitants of the city, and soon the head of Sheba is thrown over the wall, landing at the feet of Joab.

In much the same way that a trumpet call sounded the beginning of Sheba's rebellion, a trumpet call marks its end. The men of Israel who have taken refuge behind the wall of Abel Beth Maakah return to their own tents.

So ends the rebellion of Sheba, son of Bikri.

Leadership Lessons

1. The ambitious will always be willing to step into perceived leadership vacuums.

Sheba takes advantage of what he perceives to be the weakened position of David after Absalom's failed rebellion and the conflict between Judah and the other ten tribes. He raises the standard of rebellion, proclaiming, "We have no share in David" (2 Samuel 20:1). It is obvious that Sheba perceives himself to be in a position to become the leader of Israel, and is willing to exploit the opportunity.[2]

The fact that anyone follows Sheba demonstrates that there are often people who choose to follow leaders who are destined for disaster. Such leaders are often able to gather a crowd of people who are as negative, dissatisfied, and difficult to please as they are.

Ambitious men and women will always be eager to step into perceived vacuums in leadership. Drawn to power and lured by the promise of authority, some will do whatever they need to do to claim the positions to which they feel entitled. People may be willing to follow them because they are competent, but the lack of character in such leaders soon becomes apparent.

2. Some threats must be dealt with immediately and decisively.

After contending with Absalom's uprising, David becomes aware of the need to deal with rebellion swiftly. The king knows that time is of the essence. Absalom enjoyed an early success and only needed to follow it up to secure the throne. But he lost his nerve and hesitated. Absalom did not take advantage of the opportunity to crush David quickly, and David does not want to make the same mistake with Sheba.

As leaders assess threats—both outside and inside the organization—the ability to recognize which threats must be dealt with immediately and decisively is often a necessary skill for the survival of both the organization and the leader. Central to this ability is the capacity to objectively assess reality and wisely calculate consequences.

3. The defeat of one rebellion does not necessarily mean the end of all rebellion.

David may believe that he will be able to enjoy a season of peace following the end of Absalom's rebellion. That belief is short-lived.

Sheba's declaration in 2 Samuel 20:1 highlights three tenets of the rebellion. "We have no share in David" denies the king's sovereignty. Sheba claims that David has no right to reign over the ten tribes of Israel. Referring to David as "the son of Jesse" devalues the king's identity and emphasizes David's humble beginning. "Every man to his tents" draws on old tribal loyalties. Sheba is urging all who are disgruntled with David to desert him.

Leaders are not immune to criticism. Nor are they immune to hostility from those who oppose them. Leaders must address not only the overt evidences and actions of rebellion; they must also address the spirit of rebellion. Defeating the opposition and changing the mind of the opposition are two very different things. It is one thing to stop an action; it is a completely different thing to change a spirit. Changing attitudes can be far more difficult than changing behaviors. David was successful in conquering rebellion, but he doesn't defeat that spirit. In fact, he continues to deal with it the rest of his life, mostly from his own family.

4. Sometimes one wise woman can accomplish more than an army of men.

The most notable part of the passage detailing the exchange between Joab and the wise woman atop the city wall is the wisdom and resourcefulness with which the woman is able to prevent more trouble in the land. This woman of wisdom negotiates peace amid overpowering military might, and delivers her city. The peace is won at the expense of Sheba's life.

Walter Brueggemann notices the striking contrast between Joab's murderous ruthlessness and the woman's peaceable wisdom. "The wise are those not trapped in conventional perceptions. They are those who can think of an alternative way around the present set of circumstances."[3]

The wisdom of an individual can provide relief for a city. Sometimes one wise person can accomplish more than an entire army.

Questions for Leadership Development

1. What are good ways for leaders to determine which threats to the organization need to be dealt with immediately?

2. How do you deal with those in your organization who are overly ambitious?

3. What other leadership lessons can be derived from the story of Sheba?

The Psalm

Psalm 28, which could have been written by David in the midst of his troubles with Absalom and Sheba, begins with cries for help and strength. It concludes with prayers of thanksgiving for deliverance and restoration.

Psalm 28:1-7

To you, LORD, I call;
you are my Rock,
do not turn a deaf ear to me.
For if you remain silent,
I will be like those who go down to the pit.
Hear my cry for mercy
as I call to you for help,
as I lift up my hands
toward your Most Holy Place.
Do not drag me away with the wicked,
with those who do evil,
who speak cordially with their neighbors
but harbor malice in their hearts.
Repay them for their deeds
and for their evil work;
repay them for what their hands have done
and bring back on them what they deserve.
Because they have no regard for the deeds of the LORD
and what his hands have done,
he will tear them down
and never build them up again.
Praise be to the LORD,
for he has heard my cry for mercy.
The LORD is my strength and my shield;
my heart trusts in him, and he helps me.
My heart leaps for joy,
and with my song I praise him.

— SEVENTEEN —

AMASA
WHEN DELAY BECOMES DEADLY

The Background

The story of Amasa is told in 2 Samuel 17:25; 19:13; 20:1-13. He is also mentioned in 1 Kings 2:5; 2:32; 1 Chronicles 2:17.

The Story

Amasa's mother, Abigail, is the sister of David, which makes Amasa the cousin of Joab, Abishai, and Asahel, and the nephew of David.[1]

Amasa's first big career opportunity arrives when Absalom rebels against his own father, King David. Absalom recognizes the leadership ability of his cousin Amasa, and places him in command of the rebel forces that have transferred their allegiance from David to Absalom.

Following Absalom's defeat, as David begins to make his way back to Jerusalem, he sends word of his intent to replace Joab as commanding general with Amasa.[2] This action may be for political reasons: Amasa is needed to win back tribal support. Or it may be for personal reasons: Joab has fallen from the king's favor for killing Absalom. Either way, this is Amasa's second big career break, and it is intended to be a lifetime appointment. Unfortunately for Amasa, his ensuing lifetime will be brief.

Amasa's opportunity to lead David's forces comes quickly. Sheba's rebellion begins almost immediately after David signals his intent to name Amasa as commander. David is determined to deal with the troublemaker swiftly, before the uprising can gain momentum. He charges Amasa with mustering the tribe of Judah, and Amasa is given three days to accomplish the task of calling the men to arms. Unfortunately, Amasa takes longer than the allotted time to get the job done. We are not told the reason for his delay.

David, feeling immediate action is needed, instead dispatches Abishai, Joab's brother, to begin the pursuit of Sheba. Reminiscent of Abraham Lincoln's search for a general who would accomplish the objective of successfully engaging the adversary, David decisively changes generals in his search for a leader who will seize the opportunity. Abishai sets out from Jerusalem straightaway, leading Joab's men, the Kerethite and Pelethite foreign mercenaries, and all the mighty warriors in search of Sheba.

Soon after leaving Jerusalem, Abishai and the forces meet up with Amasa and the men of Judah, who are on their way back to Jerusalem to report to the king. Joab, who is accompanying Abishai, steps forward to greet Amasa. Amasa is unsuspecting of the danger at hand. "How are you, my brother?" feigns the deceitful Joab (2 Samuel 20:9). With his right hand Joab grabs his cousin's beard as if to pull Amasa forward to kiss him. Amasa does not notice the dagger in Joab's left hand. Only one thrust is needed for Joab to suddenly and savagely disembowel Amasa.[3] The deed done, Joab and Abishai immediately march off in search of Sheba.

When it becomes apparent that the gruesome sight of Amasa's eviscerated body is stopping every soldier who sees it in his tracks, one of Joab's men pulls the bloody corpse out of the middle of the road and covers it with a garment.[4]

Amasa is the third rival to meet a murderous end at the hands of Joab. The first is Abner, whom Joab murders to avenge the death of Asahel.[5] The second is Absalom, whom Joab murders while Absalom hangs helplessly from an oak tree. The third is Amasa. Both Abner and Amasa, who are better men than Joab,[6] are slain without David's knowledge. Absalom is slain despite David's specific request that the young man not be harmed.

As David nears the end of his life, he gives a charge to Solomon in which he makes reference to the murder of Amasa.[7] David reminds Solomon of how Joab killed both Abner and Amasa, two commanders of Israel's armies, "shedding their blood in peacetime as if in battle, and with that blood he stained the belt around his waist and the sandals on his feet. Deal with him according to your wisdom, but do not let his gray head go down to the grave in peace" (1 Kings 2:5-6). Amasa's murder is ultimately avenged by Benaiah, at Solomon's command.[8]

Leadership Lessons

1. Delay can be deadly.

While it is true that speed sometimes kills,[9] it is also true that delay can be deadly. It is possible to go so fast that you are dangerously out of control, but it is also possible to go so slowly, or be so late, that the opportunity for action, or even for survival, is lost.

Amasa is late. We do not know why he does not show up on time. We do know that he forfeits David's confidence when he fails to complete the task David has commissioned him to accomplish, in the timeframe that has been allotted. Amasa's leadership would make it easier for David to unify the tribes, but he fails to accomplish the task and seize the opportunity, and this failure to finish the job proves fatal.

Joab would probably attempt to kill Amasa anyway. But Amasa's delay gives Joab the ideal opportunity to act, away from the watchful eye of David and before Amasa can establish a significant following. Amasa's delay is deadly.

Leaders must have an understanding of the timeliness of opportunity and an awareness of when immediate action is of the essence. Windows of opportunity sometimes open quickly, for a limited time, and require decisive action for optimal results. It is said that Napoleon instructed his corps commanders, "You may ask me for anything you wish except time." Punctuality, promptness, and reliability will position emerging leaders for continued and greater service. The absence of such will mark them as unreliable and lacking discipline.

For leaders, delay can lead to the loss of opportunity. For Amasa, delay leads to the loss of life.

2. Promotions can make prominent targets.

After the revolt is crushed, David holds out an olive branch to Amasa by offering to appoint him as the new commander of the army. Rewarding a defeated general with leadership of the army that has been victorious over him is unusual. Replacing Joab with Amasa would be like replacing the championship-winning coach with the coach of the team he just defeated.[10]

Amasa's promotion to commander of David's forces places a big bull's-eye on his back. It is natural to assume that a military's commanding officer would be a high-value target for the enemy. It is not as likely to suspect that a military's commanding officer would become a prominent target for a cousin-in-arms.

Promotion can make you a prominent target and place you in a more vulnerable position. Leaders can become targets—not only of those on the other side but, unfortunately, also of those on their own side.

Questions for Leadership Development

1. Under what conditions might it be appropriate for promotions to be politically based rather than merit-based?

2. In what ways can a promotion be a bane rather than a blessing?

3. What other leadership lessons can be derived from the story of Amasa?

The Psalm

In Psalm 11, David speaks of the kind of evil that takes the life of a good man. David could very well have penned this psalm as he reflected on the death of honorable Amasa at the hand of vindictive Joab.

Psalm 11:5-7

The LORD examines the righteous,
but the wicked, those who love violence,
he hates with a passion.
On the wicked he will rain
fiery coals and burning sulfur;
a scorching wind will be their lot.
For the LORD is righteous,
he loves justice;
the upright will see his face.

EIGHTEEN

GAD

DEALING WITH NEGATIVE CONSEQUENCES

The Background

The story of Gad is told in 2 Samuel 24 and 1 Chronicles 21. He is also mentioned in 1 Samuel 22:5; 1 Chronicles 29:29; 2 Chronicles 29:25.

The Story

Gad is one of two prophets (the other being Nathan) who provide significant service to David. Described as both a prophet and a seer, Gad is David's personal spiritual adviser. He also records the history of David's reign.[1]

Gad is first mentioned early in David's career, while David is a fugitive from King Saul.[2] After David flees Gath and secures his parents in the safety of Moab, Gad advises David to leave the stronghold of the cave of Adullam. Rather than stay where it might be easy for Saul to trap him, Gad suggests David go to the land of Judah, where David can be among his own clan and take advantage of tribal loyalty. David heeds the valuable advice.

Gad's second (and primary) appearance takes place in the last episode recorded in 2 Samuel, when David insists on taking a count of the fighting men in Israel.

For some unspecified reason, the Lord is angry with Israel, and as a result, David is prompted to take a census.[3] There are at least three obvious reasons that a king would take a census: taxation, military conscription, or pride. None of the three reasons is appropriate. The census would most likely be viewed by the citizens as a preliminary act to the king either raising money or raising an army, and would lead to a general fear of the imposition of taxes or the establishment of a military draft. Since army officers carry out this census, the purpose is probably military in nature. The motive may simply be pride—that David wishes to know how impressive his military might really is.

In a tribal society like Israel, however, there is a fourth potential reason for a census. A census allows everyone to know the relative strength of each tribe, allowing larger tribes to demand more political power. Ambiguity in numbers forces all tribes to treat all others as equals.[4]

David instructs Joab to go throughout all Israel, from top to bottom (Dan to Beersheba), and take the census. Joab, who is not known for his sense of propriety, is nonetheless convinced of the inappropriateness of the census and tries, unsuccessfully, to talk David out of it. David insists that the count be taken, and Joab reluctantly carries out the command.

The census is accomplished in a counterclockwise sweep of the tribes and takes nine months and twenty days to complete. It indicates eight hundred thousand able-bodied men in Israel and five hundred thousand able-bodied men in Judah.[5] Because the king's directive is repulsive to him, Joab does not include the tribes of Levi and Benjamin in the numbering of the men fit for military service.

Upon receiving the results of the census, David is "conscience-stricken" (2 Samuel 24:10). He intensely regrets what he has done and immediately confesses his sin, repenting and seeking forgiveness. His prayer expresses deep contrition and remorse for his actions.

Gad comes to David the next day with a message from the Lord. God intends to punish Israel with one of three afflictions, and David is to choose which one. The options are three years of famine, three months of military defeat, or three days of plague. David is told to think the matter over and to make his decision known to Gad.

Aghast at the options, David throws himself into God's hands, believing he will fare better under the wrath of a merciful God than under the swords of ruthless men.

That very day the plague begins, and an angel is sent by God to execute the judgment. The plague takes a heavy toll, and from Dan to Beersheba, seventy thousand people die.

The wave of death sweeps across Israel, headed toward Jerusalem. As the angel is preparing to destroy Jerusalem, the Lord suddenly relents and calls for the angel to withdraw as the plague is stopped. From his vantage point in the city, David can see the angel of death reach the threshing floor of Araunah the Jebusite. With the death angel hovering over that location, David prays, begging for mercy. Still stricken in conscience, David admits again that he is at fault. Taking full responsibility for the sin, he pleads that he alone, and not the people, bear the weight of the punishment for his sin.

Gad is dispatched one final time, this time to tell David to build an altar to the Lord on Araunah's threshing floor, for it is there that the destroying angel stood when the wave of death subsided, sparing Jerusalem.

Leadership Lessons

1. Why a leader counts is as important as what a leader counts.

Joab's reluctance to complete the census may be due to a religious belief that the people belong to God and that, consequently, only God has the right to count them. David's sin is in counting something that is not appropriate for him to count.

Leaders can always find something to count, but it is important that the right things be counted. Appropriate tallying is an exercise of accountability and stewardship. For example, we know that in 1860, South Carolina produced 353,412 bales of cotton and that the figure had risen to 522,548 by 1880, and to 747,190 by 1890.[6] Taking such a careful count was deemed important for evaluating productivity and determining effectiveness and efficiency.

There is, however, a difference between counting as a matter of stewardship and counting to stoke your pride. It is one thing to count as a matter of accountability. It is another to count as an opportunity for self-promotion. The temptation is to count the things that will make the leader look good or that will provide an appearance of self-reliance.

David's numbering of the people is probably designed to show his strength as a king. If so, his sin is one of pride and of relying on the human resources at his disposal instead of relying on God.[7] In Psalm 20:7, David writes, "Some trust in chariots and some in horses, but we trust in the name of the LORD our God." If David wrote this before the census, he forgot his own words. If he wrote it after the census, it's evidence of a lesson learned.

Sometimes what really counts cannot be really counted. How can one measure the goodness of God? How can one weigh the grace of God? How can one count the mercies of God? Conversely, the easiest things to count—personal records, accomplishments, and resources—are sometimes the things least worth counting.

Pride will cause leaders to make bad decisions by counting the wrong things for the wrong reasons. In David's case, the prideful sin of counting the living results in the painful consequence of counting the dead.[8]

When leaders count, they should count the right things, for the right reasons.[9] Leaders should also recognize that what they count will likely influence how their followers behave.

2. Unaccountable authority leads to irresponsible power.

While Joab questions David's judgment in the matter of the census, David's authority to demand that his order be obeyed is unquestioned. There is no individual or group to whom he is accountable or who can overrule him. David can virtually do whatever he wants to do.

Authority that is unaccountable, combined with power that can be wielded irresponsibly, is a recipe for the abuse of leadership. Having a group of people to whom you are accountable—to whom you must answer not only for your actions but also for your motivations—is of utmost importance if a leader is going to exercise authority with integrity and credibility.

3. The repercussions of a leader's decisions can have a pronounced effect on those he or she leads.

The taking of the census brings severe consequences on unsuspecting and innocent people and results in the destruction of thousands of lives.

The account of David and the census reveals that there is a direct correlation between the actions of the leader and the effects on the people within the organization, community, or nation. The king sins, and the people die. How helpful it would be if leaders would take the time to consider the far-reaching impact of their proposed actions. How advantageous if leaders contemplated the toll in sorrow and grief that an ill-considered decision might take on others.

The Bible is filled with the reality of the consequences of sin. Charles Swindoll cautions, "If a man as great and godly as David could foul up his life so near the end of his days, so can anyone else. That includes you. That includes me. God help us all."[10]

4. God can be trusted.

David is faced with choosing one of three horrible options. His words, "Let us fall into the hands of the LORD, for his mercy is great; but do not let me fall into human hands" (2 Samuel 24:14), reveal a deep trust in God's mercy.[11]

David's decision to trust God's mercy is well founded. He trusts God in all the seasons of his life, even the painful ones. The punishment is stopped before the plague has run its course because of God's mercy.

God can be trusted. God's mercy is indeed great.

5. Prayer is an important component of leadership.

In the account of the census, David's first response to his awareness of his own sin is to pray. Without needing Gad or Nathan to convince him of his guilt, David offers two prayers. His first prayer is one of repentance.[12] He prays for himself, seeking God's forgiveness. People need to see that when their leaders sin, they seek forgiveness from God as well as from those they have wronged.

David's second prayer is one of intercession.[13] He prays for the people he serves, those who are caught in the consequences of his sin, seeking their welfare. God hears and answers David's prayer and delivers the people of Israel from the plague.

Praying for themselves and those they serve may be the most important thing leaders can do for their followers. We need leaders who pray.

Questions for Leadership Development

1. How can a leader assess the probable consequences of his or her proposed actions?

2. What are the important metrics of your leadership responsibility that really should be counted?

3. To what persons or groups are you accountable, and what is the nature of that accountability?

4. In what ways does your leadership give evidence of a trust in God?

5. What other leadership lessons can be derived from the story of Gad?

The Psalm

While many of David's psalms speak of the mercy of God, perhaps none better reflect his cry for mercy following the census
than Psalm 116. In this psalm there are overtones of distress and
mercy, and death and deliverance, all of which figure in the account of the census.

Psalm 116:1-7

I love the LORD, for he heard my voice;
he heard my cry for mercy.
Because he turned his ear to me,
I will call on him as long as I live.
The cords of death entangled me,
the anguish of the grave came over me;
I was overcome by distress and sorrow.
Then I called on the name of the LORD:
"LORD, save me!"
The LORD is gracious and righteous;
our God is full of compassion.
The LORD protects the unwary;
when I was brought low, he saved me.
Return to your rest, my soul,
for the LORD has been good to you.

— NINETEEN —

ARAUNAH
THE COST OF SACRIFICE

The Background

The story of Araunah is told in 2 Samuel 24 and 1 Chronicles 21.[1] He is also mentioned in 2 Chronicles 3:1.

The Story

Araunah owns a threshing floor located at the outskirts of Jerusalem. A Jebusite, Araunah was a citizen of the city of Jebus before David captured the city and renamed it Jerusalem.

Araunah figures prominently in the story of David's census. When David makes the ill-advised count of the fighting men of Israel, the consequence of his sin is a three-day plague that results in the death of thousands of David's subjects.

By the time the plague reaches the outskirts of Jerusalem, seventy thousand people have died. The angel is stretching out his hand to destroy Jerusalem when the Lord relents. The plague ends as the angel of death hovers over Araunah's threshing floor.

Threshing is the step in grain preparation between harvesting and winnowing and is the process of separating the hard chaff (stalks) from the grain. The next step—winnowing—separates the edible seed from the soft chaff (husk) and is most often accomplished by tossing the mixture into the air so that the wind blows away the lighter chaff while the heavier grain falls to the ground.

A threshing floor is a piece of property, usually a flattened outdoor surface, where the grain is beaten out as the seed is separated from the stalk. Threshing floors are usually on the heights, in a place exposed to the wind, in order for the winnowing process to take advantage of the breeze.

Apparently Araunah employs the traditional method of using oxen to thresh. The sheaves of grain are opened up and the stalks spread across the threshing floor. Pairs of oxen are walked over the stalks, often dragging a heavy threshing board behind them to separate the grain from the stalk and loosen the kernel from the husk.

Araunah and his four sons are at the threshing floor when the death angel approaches. Since the grain and equipment are present, it appears they are busy threshing wheat. When the angel of the Lord appears, the threshing floor becomes the place where the four sons hide in fear.[2] When the plague stops, an angel tells the prophet Gad to instruct David to build an altar to the Lord on the threshing floor of Araunah the Jebusite.

After the angel of death sheaths his sword, Araunah emerges from his hiding place. As he sees David approaching, Araunah goes out to meet him, bowing low and asking the nature of the king's visit. David responds that he has come to buy Araunah's threshing floor, that he might build an altar to the Lord in gratitude for the end of the plague.

Araunah insists on providing the king, additionally, with everything he needs to make the sacrifice. He generously offers not only the land but also the wood from his threshing sledges and ox yokes for the altar, his oxen for the burnt offering, and his wheat for the grain offering. It is unknown whether Araunah's magnanimity is due to the high esteem in which he holds King David, the fear he has of the king, or his vested interest in seeing the plague stop.

David insists on paying for the property, saying, "I will not sacrifice to the LORD my God burnt offerings that cost me nothing" (2 Samuel 24:24), and gives Araunah fifty shekels of silver.[3]

David builds the altar and prepares the sacrifice, but the fire is provided by God,[4] reminiscent of what happens when Elijah calls on God on Mount Carmel and defeats the 450 prophets of Baal and the 400 prophets of Asherah.[5]

The significance of David's purchase of Araunah's threshing floor on Mount Moriah is that it becomes the location on which Solomon builds the temple. Second Chronicles 3:1 highlights the historical significance of the property: "Then Solomon began to build the temple of the LORD in Jerusalem on Mount Moriah, where the LORD had appeared to his father David. It was on the threshing floor of Araunah the Jebusite, the place provided by David."

Leadership Lessons

1. Leaders are often called upon to model sacrifice.

David is instructed by the prophet Gad to build an altar and make a sacrifice. Though the sacrifice will benefit the entire nation, David—the leader—is the one called to make the sacrifice.

The willingness to sacrifice is an important component of leadership. In times of economic plenty, leaders usually reap the benefit and blessing of abundant resources. However, in times of economic scarcity, leaders should respond to the challenge of diminishing resources by leading the way in making sacrifices.

In his book *Spiritual Leadership*, J. Oswald Sanders has a chapter called The Cost of Leadership in which he makes this statement: "No one need aspire to leadership in the work of God who is not prepared to pay a price greater than his contemporaries and colleagues are willing to pay. True leadership always exacts a heavy toll on the whole man, and the more effective the leadership is, the higher the price to be paid."[6]

Sacrifice is integral to both leadership and worship. When sacrifice is called for, responsible leaders lead the way.

2. It is not a sacrifice unless it costs you something.

Araunah is willing to provide everything needed for David to make a sacrifice. David, however, recognizes that sacrifice requires personal cost. David's example is a good one for leaders to model today. David knows that a true sacrifice must involve significant personal expense. True sacrifice is costly.

David's sacrifice is not the last made at that location. Many sacrifices have taken place on the land known as the threshing floor of Araunah the Jebusite. Solomon constructs the temple on the site of Araunah's threshing floor, and kings and commoners offer sacrifices at that location for nearly a thousand years.

Nor is David's sacrifice the first sacrifice ever made at that location. The only other place in the Bible where Mount Moriah is mentioned is found in Genesis 22:2, where we read of another sacrifice that takes place long before King David's birth. "Then God said [to Abraham], 'Take your son, your only son, whom you love—Isaac—and go to the region of Moriah. Sacrifice him there as a burnt offering on a mountain I will show you.'"

God spares Isaac and provides in his place the sacrifice Abraham offers that day. And, centuries later, God provides the ultimate sacrifice in his Son, Jesus Christ. That sacrifice—the offering of the Son of David—is made at a cost only God can afford.

Questions for Leadership Development

1. In what ways can a leader be tempted to let other people make sacrifices the leader should be making?

2. In what ways have you benefited from a sacrificial offering made by someone else?

3. In what ways can leaders best model the example of sacrifice?

4. What other leadership lessons can be derived from the story of
   Araunah?

The Psalm

In Psalm 30, David gives thanks to God for deliverance from great danger and for God's readiness to save. He also recounts how God delivered him when he cried out for mercy. This psalm would make a fitting prayer for the dedication of David's altar and, later, of Solomon's temple, both of which stand upon the threshing floor of Araunah.

Psalm 30:1-4

A psalm. A song. For the dedication of the temple. Of David.
I will exalt you, LORD,
for you lifted me out of the depths
and did not let my enemies gloat over me.
LORD my God, I called to you for help,
and you healed me.
You, LORD, brought me up from the realm of the dead;
you spared me from going down to the pit.
Sing the praises of the LORD, you his faithful people;
praise his holy name.

— TWENTY —

RIZPAH
REAPING SOMEONE ELSE'S WHIRLWIND

The Background

The story of Rizpah is told in 2 Samuel 3:6-11; 21:1-14.

The Story

Rizpah, the daughter of Aiah, is a concubine of Saul. As such, she is provided a home and afforded a certain amount of care, but she does not have the status of a wife. From Rizpah and Saul's relationship two sons are born, Armoni and Mephibosheth.[1]

When Saul's only remaining legitimate son, Ish-Bosheth, succeeds him as king, Rizpah becomes the property of the new king. As the concubine of a previous king, she has few options, and her personal circumstances are far from ideal. Ish-Bosheth, who is insecure in his position, suspects Rizpah and Abner of indiscretions. When Ish-Bosheth accuses Abner of sleeping with Saul's concubine, Abner takes great offense to the affront and threatens to transfer his allegiance from the house of Saul to the house of David. Ish-Bosheth is aware of the tenuousness of his own position and determines it would be better to let the matter drop. The biblical text is not clear about whether Abner really has slept with Rizpah. It may be just a bad rumor making the rounds in the royal court. We also do not know what Rizpah thinks of the whole situation, but one can imagine she would be less than thrilled with the notoriety.

What Rizpah experiences some time later is a tragic tale that would rival any mother's worst nightmare. When famine strikes Israel for three successive years, David seeks divine guidance as to the reason for the calamity.[2] He learns that the famine is the result of Saul's act of putting some of the Gibeonites to death.

Centuries before, God ordered the Israelites to avoid making any covenants with people who occupied the Promised Land before the arrival of the Israelites, and to expel them from the land. By putting on worn-out clothing, the Gibeonites were able to trick Joshua and the Israelites into believing they were people from a faraway place. They were able to persuade the Israelites to make a covenant promising they would dwell in peace with the Gibeonites. The covenant resulted in Israel allowing the Gibeonites to live in their midst.[3]

David seeks "the face of the LORD" (2 Samuel 21:1) as to the cause of the famine. We are not told by what means he receives God's answer, but its content is clear: "It is on account of Saul and his blood-stained house; it is because he put the Gibeonites to death" (2 Samuel 21:1). Apparently King Saul violated the covenant made by Joshua, murdering many of the Gibeonites and planning to slaughter the rest. The Israelites had sworn to spare the Gibeonites, but Saul tried to annihilate them. Saul's attempt to eliminate the Gibeonites is not itself recorded, so we do not know the exact circumstances that have led to the famine.

Once David learns that Saul's actions are the cause of the famine, he summons the Gibeonites and asks what will atone for the atrocity that has been committed against them. They reply that they do not want monetary compensation. Instead, they require blood for blood. Since Saul is already long dead, the Gibeonites request "seven of his male descendants be given to us to be killed and their bodies exposed before the Lord at Gibeah" (2 Samuel 21:6).

David agrees to their terms.[4] He chooses to spare Mephibosheth, son of Jonathan, because of the promise he made Jonathan, but he surrenders seven of Saul's relatives, including Saul's two sons by Rizpah and five grandsons by Saul's daughter Merab. The Gibeonites kill all seven during the first days of the barley harvest, and leave their bodies exposed to the elements on a hill.

Rizpah goes to the site of the execution and spreads sackcloth[5] out for herself on a bare rock. Refusing to leave the bodies of her sons and their nephews, she stubbornly protects the corpses from molestation by wild animals by night and carrion-eating birds by day. Rizpah stays beside the bodies of her sons "from the beginning of the harvest till the rain poured down from the heavens on the bodies" (2 Samuel 21:10). After some five months the rains come, signaling that the famine is over and that Saul's sin has been forgiven.[6]

When David learns of the courage of Rizpah, the king's heart is touched by her devotion and commitment. David orders that the remains Rizpah has protected be gathered up and that the bones of Saul and his son Jonathan also be reclaimed from Jabesh-Gilead. He then gives them all an honorable burial in the family tomb of Kish, the father of Saul, in the land of Benjamin.

Rizpah is never mentioned anywhere else in the Bible, and we do not hear of her again. However, her story remains an example of love, and of loyalty and faithfulness being rewarded. Her unfailing love inspires compassion in the heart of a king. And long after the end of Israel's devastating famine, her example of devotion is still worth following.

Leadership Lessons

1. Future generations often bear the consequences of actions taken by past generations.

Saul murders many Gibeonites during his reign, attempting to annihilate them. The king is not called to account for this behavior during his lifetime, but Saul's children and grandchildren ultimately pay the price for his actions.

There is a biblical adage that is especially relevant at this point: "The parents have eaten sour grapes, and the children's teeth are set on edge" (Jeremiah 31:29). The verse highlights the maxim that one generation often reaps what the previous generation has sown. Saul's descendants end up reaping the whirlwind of the seeds of disobedience Saul himself sowed.

This is a great lesson worth remembering: Our actions affect others. Future generations can be impacted by the choices we make today. This may not be right or fair, but it is often most evident in the arenas of politics, economics, and the environment, as well as family dynamics and spiritual legacy. This truth can be evidenced when newborns bear the consequences of a parent's addictions or when a child carries the burden of a parent's unfortunate reputation.

The actions of past generations can directly impact future generations. May our children and grandchildren inherit legacies that prove to be a blessing and not a burden.

2. God expects us to honor our promises.

Saul breaks a promise made by prior generations. As king of Israel, his decisions have national implications. He represents the people who made the promise, and he breaks it.

David, however, remembers his promise to his friend Jonathan,[7] and consequently, he does not surrender Jonathan's son Mephibosheth to the Gibeonites. David honors his vow to Jonathan, even after Jonathan's death.

God expects us to honor the promises we make. In our highly self-centered culture, perhaps it would be wise for us to consider in what ways God may even expect us to honor the promises made by previous generations. God blesses the individual "who keeps an oath even when it hurts" (Psalm 15:4).

3. The influence of faithfulness is immeasurable.

Though only mentioned twice in the Bible, Rizpah demonstrates that the faithful devotion of a single individual can move the heart of a king. When her two sons are surrendered to the Gibeonites, Rizpah can do nothing to help them; all she can do is preserve their dignity in death. She abandons everyone and everything in her life, devoting herself to keeping a lonely vigil and protecting her loved ones in the only manner left to her.

After months of horror, grief, and deprivation, word of Rizpah's long vigil reaches King David, and he feels compassion for her. Though she is a woman with few rights and little power, Rizpah displays a courage and loyalty after the death of her sons that captures the attention of the king of Israel. Rizpah gives David an object lesson in faithfulness. Rizpah stands out as a woman of faithfulness in a story dominated by men who are not always faithful. Her heart-moving example of fidelity, even under hopeless and desperate conditions, influences a king.

Rizpah's story speaks to parents who have lost children, acknowledging the reality of their indescribable pain. Rizpah's months of mourning are significant and necessary, and finally lead to a time when she leaves her place of bereavement and returns to life at home.

Rizpah's tenacity and faithful devotion provide an example for all who are inclined to give up when the going gets tough. Out of loving concern she tolerates bad weather, cold, fatigue, and wild animals to protect the bodies of her dead sons. She withstands the unthinkable. Her story is tragic, her response memorable.

Leaders can learn something from Rizpah: Faithfulness is not conditioned by circumstances or fortunes. Faithfulness is an unconditional commitment to do what is right regardless of the cost or the circumstances. Faithfulness can be evidenced best in the tragic circumstances of our lives.[8]

Questions for Leadership Development

1. What tasks have you undertaken that, if you had known what was required, would have seemed beyond your ability or strength? What kept you going? What was the result?

2. When have you needed some outside circumstance to stimulate you to do what was right? What was the outcome? What would have happened if you had done nothing?

3. Who provides powerful examples of faithfulness in your context?

4. What are the promises made by past generations that you should honor?

5. What other leadership lessons can be derived from the story of Rizpah?

The Psalm

Psalm 130 is a lament in which the psalmist cries out to God in deep sorrow. The psalm reflects the kind of anguish and misery that Rizpah must have experienced. Hope finds its basis in the patient expectation of God's mercy and deliverance.

Psalm 130

Out of the depths I cry to you, LORD;
Lord, hear my voice.
Let your ears be attentive
to my cry for mercy.
If you, LORD, kept a record of sins,
Lord, who could stand?
But with you there is forgiveness,
so that we can, with reverence, serve you.
I wait for the LORD, my whole being waits,
and in his word I put my hope.
I wait for the Lord
more than watchmen wait for the morning,
more than watchmen wait for the morning.
Israel, put your hope in the LORD,
for with the LORD is unfailing love
and with him is full redemption.
He himself will redeem Israel
from all their sins.

— TWENTY-ONE —

BENAIAH
THE PEOPLE WHO SOLVE YOUR PEOPLE PROBLEMS

The Background

The story of Benaiah is told in 2 Samuel 8:18; 20:23; 23:20-22; 1 Kings 1:8-44; 2:13-25; 2:28-35; 2:36-46; 1 Chronicles 11:22-25; 18:17; 27:1-6. He is also mentioned in 1 Kings 4:4; 1 Chronicles 27:34.

The Story

Benaiah—almost always identified as "the son of Jehoiada"[1]—is a renowned warrior, famous for his storied exploits. Benaiah hails from Kabzeel and becomes the leader of the Kerethites and Pelethites who serve David. This group of elite, foreign mercenaries—essentially the Secret Service of David's day—are charged with the personal protection of King David. Their loyalty is thought to be more reliable than that of the Israelites, whose tribal allegiances might result in treachery.

Benaiah figures prominently in the listing of David's mighty men. His fame is established early in his career, when he accomplishes three heroic feats.[2] First, Benaiah single-handedly kills two of Moab's mightiest warriors. Next, he descends into a pit one snowy day and battles a lion, which he defeats.[3] Finally, Benaiah "struck down a huge Egyptian," who is seven feet six inches tall (2 Samuel 23:31). The larger, better-armed foe carries a spear that resembles a flag pole.[4] Benaiah, armed only with a club, snatches the spear from the Egyptian's hand and kills the giant with his own weapon.

Such exploits establish Benaiah's fame, assure the respect of fellow soldiers as well as foes, and guarantee him a significant place of service in David's administration. Benaiah is more famous than any of the Thirty mighty warriors. Although he is as famous as the Three elite warriors, he is not listed among them.

Officially, Benaiah holds various positions. He commands the Kerethites and Pelethites[5] and is appointed by David as chief of David's bodyguards.[6] As David's third army commander (of twelve), he is given responsibility for the military interests of Israel during the third month of each year. There are twenty-four thousand men in Benaiah's division.[7]

Benaiah proves himself a faithful supporter of both David and Solomon. He remains loyal to David when David's son Absalom rebels. When Adonijah, another son of David, makes his play for David's throne and attempts to prevent Solomon from becoming king, several of David's officials join the takeover effort. David learns of Adonijah's attempted coup and calls for Zadok the priest, Nathan the prophet, Benaiah the warrior, and the special guard to escort Solomon to Gihon, where they anoint him as king. Benaiah and the Kerethites and Pelethites provide the protective detail for Solomon's coronation.

Benaiah gives an impromptu speech when he learns of David's intent to name Solomon king: "Amen! May the LORD, the God of my lord the king, so declare it. As the LORD was with my lord the king, so may he be with Solomon to make his throne even greater than the throne of my lord King David!" (1 Kings 1:37).

Before his death, David gives Solomon instructions that include a hit list.[8] Benaiah will become instrumental in the fulfillment of those final instructions, which target Joab and Shimei.

When Adonijah discovers that David has made Solomon king, he is filled with dread and fears for his life. Solomon grants Adonijah a conditional pardon, the provision being that Adonijah pose no further threat. Adonijah soon annuls his amnesty by asking for Abishag's hand in marriage, which is viewed as a blatant second attempt to seize David's throne. Asking for Abishag, who had been King David's nurse, is the last straw. Upon learning of Adonijah's request, Solomon immediately directs Benaiah to execute the usurper.

Joab is the next to go. It is easy for the grizzled, old general to see the handwriting on the wall when he hears that Adonijah has been executed and Abiathar banished. Joab immediately flees to the tent of the LORD that David erected to house the ark of the covenant, and seeks sanctuary by grasping the horns of the altar.

Solomon directs Benaiah, "Go, strike him down!" (1 Kings 2:29).

Benaiah enters the tent of the LORD and orders Joab to leave the altar, but Joab refuses to depart: "No, I will die here" (1 Kings 2:30).

Before carrying out an execution in the tent of the LORD, Benaiah seeks further clarification from Solomon. The king's directive is succinct: "Do as he says. Strike him down and bury him, and so clear me and my whole family of the guilt of the innocent blood that Joab shed" (1 Kings 2:31). In effect, Solomon is saying, *Since he insists on staying at the altar, make a sacrifice out of him.*

Joab's murders of Abner and Amasa have not been forgotten, nor has his support of Adonijah. At Solomon's command, Benaiah puts Joab to death. The ruthless, devious commander is buried at his home in the country, perhaps in one of the barley fields that Absalom set on fire.

The last rebel to be executed by Benaiah is Shimei. Solomon has placed Shimei on parole, confining him to Jerusalem for the remainder of his life and warning him that if he ever breaks parole by leaving the city it will cost him his life. Three years later, when his slaves escape, Shimei rides his donkey over to Achish in Gath to retrieve them. Solomon soon learns of Shimei's actions, and Benaiah is once again sent to execute a dissident. With the death of Shimei accomplished, the insubordinates that so bedeviled King David are effectively eliminated and will not cause Solomon further worries. "The kingdom was now established in Solomon's hands" (1 Kings 2:46).

After Benaiah has removed those who were disloyal to the new king, Solomon appoints him to replace Joab as commander in chief of the army of Israel. Fortunately for Benaiah, whereas David's reign was marked by war, Solomon's reign is marked by peace.

Leadership Lessons

1. Like attracts like.

David's ability to attract Benaiah to a significant position of responsibility in his administration is due to the experiences and characteristics they share. David is brave and courageous, as is Benaiah. David is a warrior, as is Benaiah. David kills a lion, as does Benaiah. David has slain a giant, as has Benaiah. David is a hero, as is Benaiah.

Leaders attract followers with similar values and character. Courageous, brave, integrity-filled leaders tend to attract those who are courageous, brave, and filled with integrity. Conversely, leaders of low character and suspect morals tend to attract those of low character and suspect morals. Because of this tendency, the characteristics of the leader soon infuse and define the characteristics of the organization.

Great leaders are neither intimidated by nor resentful of the exceptional abilities and outstanding talents of others. Rather, great leaders attract great followers. All Israel reaps the benefits of the powerful partnership between David and Benaiah. Relationships like this will also make your organization stronger.

2. Mediocre leaders act only when conditions are favorable and risks are not great. Heroic leaders are willing to act even when the conditions are unfavorable and the risks are great.

In all three of the heroic exploits credited to Benaiah, the odds are stacked against him.[9] But Benaiah "met the worst of enemies, in the worst of places, under the worst of conditions; and he won."[10]

Courageous leaders realize they cannot wait for the perfect sunny day to battle a lion or tackle a dangerous problem. There are situations in our lives that cannot wait. Mediocre leaders prefer to wait until conditions are posh, plush, and painless; but pits can be deep, dark, and deadly. Heroic leaders overcome great odds, great obstacles, and great opponents, even during poor conditions.

When courage (the willingness to act despite bad conditions) meets wisdom (the ability to know when action is immediately necessary), heroic leaders are produced. Heroic leaders face overwhelming odds at great personal risk, and achieve exploits that are seldom achieved by those whose primary concern is their own personal comfort or convenience. Heroic leaders are those willing to act even when conditions are not favorable. Heroic leaders fight the battles they have, not the battles they wish they had.

3. Heroic exploits are often a precursor to significant service.

If you were looking for a bodyguard—someone you could trust implicitly with your own well-being—what qualifications would you consider important? You would probably not be looking for a person who simply had security training, or who had only interned with a protection company. On the other hand, the résumé of a person who has killed an Egyptian giant and slain a lion in a pit on a snowy day would probably make it to the top of your stack of candidates. Benaiah's courageous exploits position him for the opportunity to provide significant service to the king and the kingdom. Benaiah's heroism qualifies him to command the elite corps of foreign mercenaries who serve as David's guards.

Men and women of courage and quality will usually find their names at the top of the list when leaders are looking for individuals to provide important service for an organization.

4. Your team should include people who are gifted in resolving people problems.

Benaiah is obviously effective at helping with David's people problems. David died of natural causes at a good, old age. No one assassinated him. So far as we know, no one even physically harmed him. Benaiah does his job well.

Benaiah then becomes proficient at handling Solomon's people problems. In fact, he completely eliminates both the problems and the people. Benaiah becomes Solomon's enforcer. He enables Solomon to firmly establish his authority and to govern without significant opposition.

Leaders have always dealt with people problems, and they always will. The human relations issues you and I face obviously need to be handled differently than Solomon handled his issues. However, leaders often need assistance from individuals who are gifted in handling people problems. In the same way that Solomon looks to Benaiah to set right difficult personnel situations, leaders today are wise to seek help from others. Leaders need team members with significant relational skills who can help them navigate people problems. Wise leaders recruit such valuable individuals to their organizations then give them the authority to act in ways that are appropriate and effective.

Questions for Leadership Development

1. What kind of associates does your leadership tend to attract?

2. Who are the people you turn to when you need help with people problems?

3. What other leadership lessons can be derived from the story of Benaiah?

The Psalm

Psalm 91 is commonly known as the Warrior's Psalm. Perhaps David had Benaiah in mind when he wrote these words that have brought comfort to many a soldier. The assurance of God's protection for those who are in harm's way is vital to their confidence and hope.

Psalm 91:1-10

Whoever dwells in the shelter of the Most High
will rest in the shadow of the Almighty.
I will say of the Lord, "He is my refuge and my fortress,
my God, in whom I trust."
Surely he will save you
from the fowler's snare
and from the deadly pestilence.
He will cover you with his feathers,
and under his wings you will find refuge;
his faithfulness will be your shield and rampart.
You will not fear the terror of night,
nor the arrow that flies by day,
nor the pestilence that stalks in the darkness,
nor the plague that destroys at midday.
A thousand may fall at your side,
ten thousand at your right hand,
but it will not come near you.
You will only observe with your eyes
and see the punishment of the wicked.
If you say, "The Lord is my refuge,"
and you make the Most High your dwelling,
no harm will overtake you,
no disaster will come near your tent.

AFTERWORD
A MAN AFTER GOD'S OWN HEART

"Then the people asked for a king, and he gave them Saul son of Kish, of the tribe of Benjamin, who ruled forty years. After removing Saul, he made David their king. God testified concerning him: 'I have found David son of Jesse, a man after my own heart; he will do everything I want him to do.'

"From this man's descendants God has brought to Israel the Savior Jesus, as he promised.

"…Now when David had served God's purpose in his own generation, he fell asleep; he was buried with his ancestors and his body decayed. But the one whom God raised from the dead did not see decay."

—Acts 13:21-23, 36-37

When you mention David, most people make a connection, and the connection usually takes them back to someone in David's story. Many people link David to the giant Goliath, or to Bathsheba, the wife of Uriah, or to David's classic friendship with Jonathan.

When the apostle Paul thinks of David, the connection he makes does not take him back to someone in David's story. Rather, the connection moves Paul forward, to Jesus.

Paul's sermon in Acts 13 is directed to a primarily Jewish audience at Pisidian Antioch. A key component of Paul's message is a brief survey of Israel's history, and the rise of David is prevalent in Paul's historical retrospect. The historical introduction, however, only serves to pave the way for Jesus. For Paul, David is the link between Israel's history and the coming of the Messiah, Jesus Christ. Paul shows how Jesus is the Messiah promised by David, predicted by the prophets, and foretold by John the Baptist. As a descendant of David, Jesus is the fulfillment of prophecy. That day at Pisidian Antioch, the heart of Paul's message is that, from David's seed, God has raised up a Savior, Jesus.

Paul's listeners hold David in high esteem. By the time the New Testament is written, David's enduring legacy is well established. He unified twelve scattered tribes into a nation. He established a kingdom. He was a great leader. Most significant, the Bible states that David was a man after God's own heart.

As a man after God's heart, David displays trust and confidence in God. This is seen early in the story of David, when he battles Goliath. His confidence in God is also evidenced when David has the opportunity on at least two occasions to kill Saul and take the throne of Israel. Yet he refuses to harm the Lord's anointed, preferring to allow God to choose when he will become king.

As a man after God's heart, David has a love and respect for the Scriptures, which teach him how to draw closer to God. David writes, "I meditate on your precepts and consider your ways. I delight in your decrees; I will not neglect your word" (Psalm 119:15-16). "Your word is a lamp for my feet, a light on my path" (Psalm 119:105). These passages reflect David's appreciation for divine instruction.

As a man after God's heart, David worships God with abandon. His praise and exaltation when the ark of the covenant is brought to Jerusalem show that his heart blazes for God.

As a man after God's heart, David responds with confession and repentance when confronted with his own sins, most notably in the story of Bathsheba and in his taking of the census.

However, as one gains a comprehensive awareness of David's life, Acts 13:22 becomes troublesome. The words Paul attributes to God—"I have found David son of Jesse, a man after my own heart; he will do everything I want him to do"—are problematic. While David may do everything God wants him to do, he also does some things God does not want him to do.

John Wesley's comments on Acts 13 are illuminating:

I have found David, a man after mine own heart. This expression is to be taken in a limited sense. David was such at that time, but not at all times: and he was so in that respect, as he performed all God's will in the particulars there mentioned. But he was not a man after God's own heart in other respects, wherein he performed his own will. In the matter of Uriah, for instance, he was as far from being a man after God's heart as Saul himself was. It is therefore a very gross, as well as dangerous, mistake to suppose this is the character of David in every part of his behavior. We must beware of this, unless we would recommend adultery and murder as things after God's own heart.[1]

David is flawed, sometimes in significant ways. He sins, and his sins include murder and adultery. Yet, when confronted with his sins, David responds in ways that evidence remorse, humility, confession, and repentance. Despite his transgressions, it is his response to his own conviction of personal sin that allows him to serve God's purposes in his own generation.

David learns to care about the things God cares about. He longs for God like a thirsty deer longs for a drink of water. His heart beats in sync with God's heart. He pays attention to the things God considers important. He learns what pleases God and what disappoints God, and his desire to please God becomes paramount.

Like David, the leaders of today are called to lead with hearts after God's own heart in order to serve God's purpose in their own generation. Such leaders will recognize the importance of the orientation and purity of their own hearts. Such leaders will possess not only competence but also character. We desperately need such leaders—men and women who possess both ability and integrity.

While attending a recent theology conference, I had the privilege of participating in discussion with a small group whose members represented seven nations and four continents. One topic of discussion in the group was the particular organization of the Nazarene denomination, and whether the structure is conducive to mission achievement. One participant made the observation that the specific structure of an organization is not the most important factor in mission achievement. Rather, the most important factor is the character of the hearts of the organization's leaders. When it comes to ecclesiastical effectiveness, if the hearts of the leaders are not right, good, holy, and pure, the institution is destined for futility. The same is true of organizational effectiveness. If the hearts of the organization's leaders do not reflect purity and character, that institution or organization is ultimately destined for failure.

Many of today's leaders are flawed, sometimes in substantial ways. They have shortcomings. They make significant mistakes. The one hope we have for the Christian leaders of this generation and the next is that their longing for God will be a compass that orients them toward righteousness, justice, and holy character, so that when course corrections, attitude adjustments, and behavioral changes are needed, it is this longing for God that will allow the Holy Spirit to continually transform their hearts.

When heart transformation happens—when leaders have hearts after God's own heart—those leaders become men and women who serve God's purposes in their own generations. Even more importantly than leading with "skillful hands," these leaders lead with "integrity of heart."[2] May you and I be such leaders.

APPENDIX
LEADERSHIP LESSONS BY CHAPTER

Chapter 1. Ahimelek: Slaughter of the Innocents

1. You can tell a lot about people by where they go in times of trouble.
2. Religious rituals can either be obstacles to or opportunities for meeting human needs.
3. There is sometimes a price to be paid for innocent kindness.
4. There are people in this world who are "hopelessly committed to evil intentions."
5. If all those closest to you think your decision is wrong, you should rethink your decision.

Chapter 2. Josheb-Basshebeth: Daleph Force Three

1. Stories of past struggles and victories can create the ethos and shape the identity of an organization.
2. Leaders must sometimes stand alone, even if on a great team.
3. Some acts of bravery and service become sacrifices of which only God is worthy.
4. Leaders acknowledge when victory is the result of God's supernatural blessing.

Chapter 3. Amasai: Pick Your Partners Carefully

1. When considering potential partners, leaders should clearly articulate their expectations.
2. Leaders know the difference between the ends and the means.

Chapter 4. Asahel: When Speed Kills

1. Beware, lest your adversary use your strength against you.
2. Beware, lest your momentum carry you to catastrophe.
3. Beware the potential consequences of the action you are contemplating.

Chapter 5. Uzzah: Doing the Right Thing the Wrong Way

1. It is possible for leaders to cross the line.
2. The great enemy of obedience is convenience.
3. God can take care of himself.
4. The right things need to be done the right way.

Chapter 6. Obed-Edom: The Cycle of Blessing and Responsibility

1. Faithful leaders often experience cycles of blessing and responsibility, leading to increased blessing and increased responsibility.
2. Responsible service can become a family affair.

Chapter 7. Amnon: Family Feud

1. A leader's sins have the propensity to permeate the culture of an organization, institution, or family.
2. When leaders encounter injustice, they can respond in ways that either end it or perpetuate it.
3. Most moral problems, if ignored, breed further issues.
4. First reports are rarely entirely accurate.

Chapter 8. Tamar: Am I My Sister's Keeper?

1. Anyone can become a victim of violence.
2. Victims of violence need leaders who will listen to their stories, believe them, and take appropriate action.
3. There are two kinds of family trouble: trouble from without and trouble from within.

Chapter 9. Jonadab: Beware the Instigator

1. Beware of those "eager to put their wits to the service of other people's evil."
2. The character of the adviser is often indicative of the quality of the advice.

Chapter 10. Ahithophel: To Whom Do You Listen?

1. The unfaithfulness of leaders often results in the disloyalty of followers.
2. The ability to discern whose advice to follow is critical to a leader's success.

Chapter 11. Hushai: Even a King Needs a Friend

1. There is a difference between a counselor and a confidant.
2. When it comes to strategy, simple is often preferred over complicated.
3. There is nothing like a crisis to help leaders clearly identify their friends and enemies.
4. God's ultimate plan will not be thwarted.

Chapter 12. Ittai the Gittite: Who's By Your Side?

1. "A real friend is one who walks in when others walk out."
2. It is possible for your enemy to become your ally.
3. The reward for great loyalty is great trust.

Chapter 13. Shimei: The Exhausting Effect of Criticism

1. When facing criticism, keep moving.
2. When facing criticism, respond with grace and humility.
3. When facing criticism, find ways to refresh yourself.
4. When giving criticism, remember that words have consequences.

Chapter 14. Barzillai: The Importance of Supply Lines

1. Do not underestimate the importance of supply lines.
2. A loyal friend is a priceless treasure.

3. Your children may be the ones who most benefit from your kindness to others.

Chapter 15. Ahimaaz: Good Man; Good News

1. In order to make good decisions, it is important to have good information.
2. Good people are often known for bringing good news.
3. It sometimes makes sense to take a different route than others are taking.
4. Motivation will often outdistance talent.

Chapter 16. Sheba: Of Ambition and Rebellion

1. The ambitious will always be willing to step into perceived leadership vacuums.
2. Some threats must be dealt with immediately and decisively.
3. The defeat of one rebellion does not necessarily mean the end of all rebellion.
4. Sometimes one wise woman can accomplish more than an army of men.

Chapter 17. Amasa: When Delay Becomes Deadly

1. Delay can be deadly.
2. Promotions can make prominent targets.

Chapter 18. Gad: Dealing with Negative Consequences

1. Why a leader counts is as important as what a leader counts.
2. Unaccountable authority leads to irresponsible power.
3. The repercussions of a leader's decisions can have a pronounced effect on those he or she leads.
4. God can be trusted.
5. Prayer is an important component of leadership.

Chapter 19. Araunah: The Cost of Sacrifice

1. Leaders are often called upon to model sacrifice.
2. It is not a sacrifice unless it costs you something.

Chapter 20. Rizpah: Reaping Someone Else's Whirlwind

1. Future generations often bear the consequences of actions taken by past generations.
2. God expects us to honor our promises.
3. The influence of faithfulness is immeasurable.

Chapter 21. Benaiah: The People Who Solve Your People Problems

1. Like attracts like.
2. Mediocre leaders act only when conditions are favorable and risks are not great. Heroic leaders are willing to act even when the conditions are unfavorable and the risks are great.
3. Heroic exploits are often a precursor to significant service.
4. Your team should include people who are gifted in resolving people problems.

NOTES

Chapter 1

1. There is some confusion created by 2 Samuel 8:17 and 1 Chronicles 18:16; 24:3, 24:6, and 24:31. It may be that these passages accidentally transpose the names of Ahimelek and Abiathar. Or, perhaps both Abiathar's father and Abiathar's son were named Ahimelek.

2. See 1 Samuel 14:3.

3. Kevin J. Mellish suggests, "Because of his ties to Saul, David may have been unsure whether he could trust Ahimelek and therefore had to disguise his intentions." *1 & 2 Samuel: A Commentary in the Wesleyan Tradition, New Beacon Bible Commentary* (Kansas City: Beacon Hill Press of Kansas City, 2012), 140.

4. The significance of David requesting exactly five loaves of bread is unknown. It may simply indicate that David is telling the truth in 1 Samuel 21:2, when he tells Ahimelek his men are meeting him elsewhere. Jesus's statement in Matthew 12:3-4 gives veracity to this part of David's claim. It is interesting to note, though, that David also picks up five stones when he faces Goliath.

5. See Leviticus 24:5-9.

6. Robert Alter observes, "This is the second reference in this narrative to a general practice of refraining from sexual activity during periods of combat." *The David Story: A Translation with Commentary of 1 and 2 Samuel* (New York: W. W. Norton and Company, Inc., 1999), 132.

Mellish suggests, "Being clean probably meant that the soldiers had to abstain from sexual intercourse before a battle (Exodus 19:15)." *1 & 2 Samuel,* 140.

7. The Bible does not tell how Goliath's sword got from David's tent (see 1 Samuel 17:54) to the sanctuary at Nob. Nor does it reveal what happens to the sword after David retrieves it at Nob.

8. Walter Brueggemann notes that Ahimelek's defense of David is fourfold: David is known to be reliable. David is the king's son-in-law. David holds high military office. David is honored at court. Also, in his own defense, Ahimelek avows that he has provided priestly functions for David

on previous occasions without questions being raised. *First and Second Samuel: Interpretation, A Bible Commentary for Teaching and Preaching* (Louisville: John Knox Press, 1990), 159.

9. The slaughter of Ahimelek and the other eighty-four priests at Nob calls to mind the prophecy made against the house of Eli in 1 Samuel 2:27-36.

10. Bill T. Arnold notes, "You can learn a lot about a person by seeing where they turn in times of trouble." *1 & 2 Samuel: The NIV Application Commentary* (Grand Rapids: Zondervan, 2003), 310.

11. This memorable phrase is used by Arnold, *1 & 2 Samuel,* 313.

12. See 1 Samuel 22:6-13, where, rather than calling him by name, Saul consistently refers to David as "son of Jesse."

13. Jonathan Kirsch notes that there have been many times that those in power have "resorted to terror and even mass murder to discourage a local populace from sheltering an enemy and to make an example of those who are suspected of doing so. Nob is only the first in a list that includes Lidice, the Czech town that Nazi Germany eradicated as a punishment for harboring partisans in World War II; Dier Yassin, the Arab village that was terrorized by the Irgun and the Stern Gang in the War of Independence that brought the modern state of Israel into existence; and My Lai, the Vietnamese village where civilians were slaughtered out of fear and hatred of the Vietcong." *King David: The Real Life of the Man Who Ruled Israel* (New York: Ballantine Books, 2000), 87.

14. John Wesley, *Explanatory Notes upon the Old Testament,* Vol. II (Salem, OH: Schmul Publishers, 1975), 963.

Chapter 2

1. In 1 Chronicles 11:11, 12:6, and 27:2, Josheb-Basshebeth is referred to as Jashobeam.

2. Abishai is later identified as their chief in 2 Samuel 23:18-19, though—inexplicably—is explicitly not counted among the Three.

3. See Cliff Graham's book *Day of War,* the first in his *Lion of War* series, for a gripping, fictional account based on the exploits of David and his Mighty Men (*Day of War,* Grand Rapids: Zondervan, 2011).

4. Hence the chapter title, "Daleph Team Three." Daleph is the fourth letter of the Hebrew alphabet and corresponds to the Greek letter Delta.

5. This is a term Bill T. Arnold uses in describing 2 Samuel 23. *1 & 2 Samuel: The NIV Application Commentary* (Grand Rapids: Zondervan, 2003), 636.

6. The account in 1 Chronicles 11:11 indicates Josheb-Basshebeth killed only three hundred men.

7. See Judges 15:15-17.

8. See 1 Chronicles 27:2.

9. "Remember the Alamo!" became the battle cry of Texans fighting for their independence from Mexico. The words called to mind the courage of the soldiers who were massacred by Mexican forces at the Alamo in San Antonio in March 1836.

"Forty Rounds!" is the motto of the U.S. Army 13th Infantry Regiment, presently stationed at Fort Jackson, Columbia, SC. The motto became a greeting by members of the unit following an incident during the Civil War, when a soldier of the 13th was asked about the location of the identifying corps badge or insignia on his uniform (the unit had none). The soldier replied by tapping his cartridge box and saying, "Forty rounds in the cartridge box and twenty in the pocket!"

"No Ground to Give!" is the motto of the 193rd Infantry Brigade, presently stationed at Fort Jackson, Columbia, SC. The motto originated from the brigade's involvement in Operation Just Cause in Panama, when tasked with defending terrain that was so limited, with options for repositioning so restricted, that there was literally "no ground to give."

10. Uttered by Martin Luther when he faced the emperor of the Holy Roman Empire at Worms. Luther's stand initiated Protestantism.

11. See Ecclesiastes 4:12.

12. Arnold, *1 & 2 Samuel,* 640.

13. Walter Brueggemann, *First and Second Samuel: Interpretation, A Bible Commentary for Teaching and Preaching* (Louisville: John Knox Press, 1990), 349.

14. Brueggemann, *First and Second Samuel,* 349.

15. Brueggemann, *First and Second Samuel,* 347.

16. Arnold, *1 & 2 Samuel,* 639.

Chapter 3

1. These mighty men, like the Three, are an elite group of David's toughest warriors, all of whom are credited with heroic feats of valor.

2. Another Amasai mentioned in the Bible is apparently a contemporary of the Amasai who is chief of the Thirty. The other Amasai, referred to in 1 Chronicles 15:24, is a Levite, while the chief of the Thirty is from the tribe of either Judah or Benjamin.

Chapter 4

1. This story highlights what Jonathan Kirsch refers to as "the highly personal nature of combat in the ancient world, and, especially, the terrible intimacy of war." *King David* (New York: Ballantine Books, 2000), 138.

2. Kevin Mellish notes, "Asahel's speed was matched only by his determination to overtake Abner." *1 & 2 Samuel*, 187.

3. I am indebted to Joe McLamb for this insight.

4. Walter Brueggemann notes, "Asahel is fast, but that is all. He is impetuous and foolish." *First and Second Samuel*, 222.

Chapter 5

1. See Bill T. Arnold, *1 & 2 Samuel*, 459.

2. As Walter Brueggemann notes, "The ark embodies what is unifying among the tribes and clans of Israel." *First and Second Samuel*, 248.

3. Baalah is called Kiriath Jearim in 1 Chronicles 13:5.

4. C. S. Lewis, *The Chronicles of Narnia: The Lion, the Witch and the Wardrobe* (New York: Harper Collins, 1994), 80.

5. Eugene H. Peterson notes, "Uzzah is the patron saint of those who uncritically embrace technology without regard to the nature of the Holy." *First and Second Samuel* (Louisville: John Knox Press, 1999), 163.

6. Peterson, *First and Second Samuel*, 163.

7. For an outstanding sermon (with a powerful ending) on Uzzah, by Craig Barnes, President of Princeton Theological Seminary, please reference http://wowza.ptsem.edu/storage/2014/BarnesSermon042814/8794V_cb042814.mp3. Last accessed September 17, 2015.

Chapter 6

1. A certain amount of confusion is attached to Obed-Edom. He is referred to as "the Gittite" in 2 Samuel 6:10-11, which has caused much confusion. The designation "the Gittite" may mean that Obed-Edom is a native of Gath, a Philistine city. Eugene Peterson (*First and Second Samuel*, 163) and Kevin Mellish (*1 & 2 Samuel*, 205) are two of the few who make this claim.

Among many others, Joyce G. Baldwin suggests that it is unlikely that Obed-Edom is a Philistine, and is probably a Levite because he is entrusted with the ark. "At least three Israelite towns had names compounded with Gath, from one of which this man originally came." *1 and 2 Samuel: An Introduction and Commentary, Tyndale Old Testament Commentaries*, (Downers Grove, IL: InterVarsity Press, 1988), 223.

Since Obed-Edom is a Levite (see 1 Chronicles 15:16-18), this "Gittite" is probably from Gath-Rimmon in the territory of Dan and Manasseh, which is assigned to the Kohathite clan of the Levites (see Joshua 21:24-25, 1 Chronicles 26:1-4).

2. Kevin Mellish notes, "It is possible to conclude that blessing Obed-Edom's household was a sign to David he did not have to fear the terrifying power of the ark if it was handled in the proper way." *1 & 2 Samuel*, 205-206.

3. See 1 Chronicles 26:6.

Chapter 7

1. It may be that Absalom's initial plan is more far-reaching than just the assassination of Amnon. Eugene Peterson suggests that Absalom's goal may be to kill both his father, David, and all his brothers, in order to secure the throne. When David declines the invitation, Absalom has to settle for Amnon (*First and Second Samuel*, 196). It is hard to imagine that Absalom would assassinate Amnon in the presence of David, though. It is even harder to imagine that David does not suspect that Absalom's taking of Amnon's life is not only for personal reasons of vengeance but also for political reasons of succession. Absalom would be well aware that the death of Amnon would move him up in the line of succession.

2. Bill T. Arnold notes, "The king was guilty of sexual transgression and murder, both of which come back to haunt him here among his own children." *1 & 2 Samuel*, 568.

3. See Brueggemann, *First and Second Samuel*, 287-288, and Arnold, *1 & 2 Samuel*, 559-569.

Chapter 8

1. Kevin Mellish notes that as a virgin in the king's household, "Tamar may have been chaperoned, making it difficult for Amnon to carry out his carnal intentions." *1 & 2 Samuel*, 239.

2. "Why take me by force when you can enjoy me legitimately?" Alter, *The David Story*, 268.

3. See 2 Samuel 13:20. See Alter, 270.

4. See 2 Samuel 13:15-17.

5. Kirsch, *King David*, 216.

6. Bill T. Arnold suggests that Tamar's richly ornamented robe "signified her status as an unmarried princess (2 Samuel 13:18). Once she tears it, the robe symbolizes the ruin of her life." *1 & 2 Samuel*, 564.

7. Tamar's "coat of many colors" is strikingly similar to distinctive clothing Joseph wears in Genesis 37. Both robes signify special favor. Both Tamar and Joseph are abandoned, disgraced, and humiliated. Both articles of clothing become torn, and most likely both are bloodied. For a more detailed comparison, see Adrien Janis Bledstein's "Tamar and the 'Coat of Many Colors'" (Athalya Brenner, ed. *A Feminist Companion to Samuel & Kings* [Sheffield, UK: Sheffield Academic Press, 2000], 65-85).

8. See 2 Samuel 13:20.

9. See 2 Samuel 14:27.

10. "All too often, survivors of violence are re-traumatized by pastors and other well-meaning helpers who press forgiveness upon them as if it were something which, if they tried hard enough, they could simply will into happening. If the survivor tries to forgive, she can only fail, and her failure will reinforce all the self-blame and shame of her original abuse." Pamela Cooper-White, *The Cry of Tamar: Violence Against Women and the Church's Response* (Minneapolis: Fortress Press, 1995), 253.

11. Artists have often attempted to tell the story of Tamar's rape. For an intriguing treatment of the rape of Tamar in Baroque art, see Sara Kipfer's article in The Society of Biblical Literature, http://www.sbl-site.org/publications/article.aspx?ArticleId=800. Last accessed September 18, 2015. Kipfer suggests that the subject was a favored theme of sixteenth- and seventeenth-century Italian and Dutch painters and is depicted in no fewer than twenty paintings and probably also in as many copper engravings and woodcuts.

12. Charles R. Swindoll, *David: A Man of Passion and Destiny* (Nashville: Thomas Nelson, 2000), 347.

13. Robert Pinsky observes of Amnon's attack of Tamar, "This familial rape tears the fabric of life apart in a widening, accelerated gash." *The Life of David* (New York: Random House, 2005), 123.

14. Swindoll says that David "had too many wives and too many children to lead and rear properly." *David*, 226.

15. Peterson notes that this is "the first installment of Nathan's prophesied consequences of David's sin against Bathsheba and Uriah." *First and Second Samuel*, 191. See 2 Samuel 12:11.

Chapter 9

1. See 2 Samuel 13:35.

2. Peterson, *First and Second Samuel*, 192.

3. Peterson observes, "The intelligence and imagination that is generated daily in the cause of assisting others to acquire illegitimate power and indulge wrongful pleasure is astounding." *First and Second Samuel,* 192.

4. I am indebted to Joe McLamb for this insight.

5. See 1 Kings 12:1-24.

6. I am indebted to Scott Estep for this insight.

Chapter 10

1. An example of this is seen when executives who enjoy profit-sharing perks defer prudent maintenance expenses so they can enjoy larger bonus checks based on the organization's larger year-end cash balances. The result is that leaders reap short-term benefits while the organization suffers long-term consequences.

Chapter 11

1. Brueggemann observes, "It is possible for otherwise sober people to embrace war strategies that are as remote from reality as the plan of Hushai. Our own history tells us that war councils are not simply forums of reason but struggles between massive egos, partisan interests, and much fantasy." *First and Second Samuel,* 312.

Chapter 12

1. Peterson, *First and Second Samuel,* 209.

2. See Matthew 1:5-6.

3. This quote is attributed to Walter Winchell.

Chapter 13

1. See Exodus 6:17; Numbers 3:18; 1 Chronicles 3:19; 4:26-27; 5:4; 6:17; 6:29; 6:42; 8:21; 23:7-10; 25:3; 25:17; 27:27; 2 Chronicles 29:14; 31:12-13; Ezra 10:23; 10:33; 10:38; Esther 2:5; Zechariah 12:13.

2. Alexander Whyte calls Shimei "a reptile of the royal house of Saul." *Bible Characters,* (Grand Rapids: Zondervan, 1952), 297.

3. One reason Solomon gives Shimei a second chance may be because Shimei did not join Adonijah's play for the throne. See 1 Kings 1:8.

4. The conclusion of the account of Shimei furnishes a practical example of how Israel's cities of refuge work. They provide a safe haven as long as the accused resides therein but afford no protection beyond their borders.

5. As Swindoll observes, "The humbled forgiven make good forgivers." *David,* 431.

6. Swindoll notes, "Most of us would rather sit on a judgment seat than a mercy seat." *David*, 420.

7. I am indebted to Scott Estep for this insight.

Chapter 14

1. The precise location of Mahanaim is uncertain. It is probably in the same general area as Jabesh-Gilead, somewhere east of the Jordan River, near the Jabbok River.

2. Kimham is assumed by most interpreters to be one of Barzillai's younger sons. See Arnold, *1 & 2 Samuel*, 601. See 1 Kings 2:6.

3. Peterson writes, "In the murk and tangle of mixed motives and ne-gotiated advantages that have clustered at the Jordan, this scene gives the last word to free generosity, to the grace of hospitality—a rare moment in David's life, and all the more to be treasured in that everything in David's world is soon to disintegrate again into rivalry and self-seeking and vio-lence." *First and Second Samuel*, 234.

4. See 1 Kings 2:7.

5. Swindoll observes, "Centuries later, here is David out in the middle of nowhere. Mahanaim and the angels come in the form of three men who bring them all the food and supplies that they need out there in the wilderness." *David*, 409.

6. I am indebted to Joe McLamb for this insight.

Chapter 15

1. Peterson, *First and Second Samuel*, 224.

2. Arnold, *1 & 2 Samuel*, 596.

3. The Cushite runs the most difficult route "through the tangled forest of Ephraim, back to Mahanaim." Peterson, *First and Second Samuel*, 224.

Alter suggests that the plain in question in 2 Samuel 18:23 is the east side of the Jordan Valley, which is a flatter, if less direct, route (*The David Story*, 308).

4. Kirsch suggests that the sight of "many men on the run was a sign of an army in rout, but a single runner meant only that a message had been sent from the front." *King David*, 249.

5. It may be that Ahimaaz, son of Zadok, is the same Ahimaaz who marries Basemath, daughter of Solomon, and who becomes Solomon's dis-trict governor in Naphtali. See 1 Kings 4:15.

6. I am indebted to Joe McLamb for this insight.

Chapter 16

1. See Pinsky, *The Life of David*, 154, 163-164.

2. "Such rebellion," writes Arnold, "is accomplished in the dark among conniving miscreants, who rely on secrecy and trickery to acquire power." *1 & 2 Samuel,* 610.

3. Brueggemann, *First and Second Samuel,* 331-332.

Chapter 17

1. According to 2 Samuel 17:25, Amasa's father is Ithra the Israelite, but Jether the Ishmaelite is said to be his father in 1 Chronicles 2:17.

2. See 2 Samuel 19:13.

3. Brueggemann's concise description matches the briefness of the confrontation: "Swiftly, silently, and mercilessly, Joab has eliminated his rival." *First and Second Samuel,* 331.

4. Kirsch suggests, "Only then did the reluctant men of the tribal muster begin to put one foot in front of the other and move off numbly after Joab." *King David,* 258.

5. See chapter 4.

6. See 1 Kings 2:32.

7. See 1 Kings 2:5.

8. See 1 Kings 2:28-34.

9. See chapter 4.

10. Brueggemann suggests, "The political risk in displacing Joab must have been something like the risk for President Truman in dismissing General MacArthur from his Pacific command. Surely Joab will not take the dismissal lightly." *First and Second Samuel,* 326.

Chapter 18

1. See 1 Chronicles 29:29.

2. See 1 Samuel 22:5.

3. 2 Samuel 24:1 attributes the prompting to God, while 1 Chronicles 21:1 suggests that Satan is directly responsible for impressing David's mind with the temptation.

4. I am indebted to Joe McLamb for this insight.

5. See 2 Samuel 24:9. First Chronicles 21:5-6 lists the results of the census as 1,100,000 troops, including 470,000 in Judah, but this figure does not include the tribes of Levi and Benjamin. The data is presented in an interesting way, implying that Judah is by far the largest tribe, and that the other tribes can counterbalance Judah only by forming a coalition—which they do.

6. Walter Edgar, *South Carolina: A History* (Columbia, SC: University of South Carolina Press, 1998), 428.

7. As Peterson observes, "Counting soldiers is the opposite of trusting in God." *First and Second Samuel,* 263.

8. Pinsky observes the irony of "counting the dead who died as retribution for counting the living." *The Life of David,* 170.

9. For insights on what churches should be counting, see Ed Stetzer's article: http://www.churchleaders.com/pastors/pastor-articles /244451-counting-correctly-create-right-scorecard-churches.html?utm _source=newsletter&utm_medium=email&utm_campaign=clnewslet ter&utm_content=CL+Daily+20150102. Last accessed September 29, 2015.

10. Swindoll, *David,* 471.

11. Brueggemann observes, "At his best, David fears God the most. He also trusts God the most." *First and Second Samuel,* 353.

12. See 2 Samuel 24:10.

13. See 2 Samuel 24:17.

Chapter 19

1. In some versions (KJV, NASB), Araunah is called Ornan in 1 Chronicles 21:18-28.

2. See 1 Chronicles 21:20.

3. In 1 Chronicles 21:25-26, the payment is listed as six hundred shekels of gold. Robert L. Sawyer explains the difference by suggesting that the price of fifty shekels of silver mentioned in 2 Samuel 24 includes the oxen, materials for the sacrifice, and threshing floor, while the amount listed in 1 Chronicles 21 includes all of the materials in addition to both the threshing floor itself and the entire surrounding area upon which the temple is to be constructed. *Beacon Bible Commentary,* Vol. 2 (Kansas City: Beacon Hill Press of Kansas City, 1965), 330, 544-545.

4. See 1 Chronicles 21:25.

5. See 1 Kings 18:16-40.

6. J. Oswald Sanders, *Spiritual Leadership* (Chicago: Moody Press, 1969), 169.

Chapter 20

1. Not to be confused with Mephibosheth, son of Jonathan.

2. There is no way to know exactly when the three-year famine takes place. Arnold suggests, "The slaughter of the sons of Saul may be implied in the words of Shimei (2 Samuel 16:8), which would mean the famine and the execution of Saul's descendants occurred prior to Absalom's revolt" (*1 & 2 Samuel,* 619).

3. See Joshua 9.

4. Some commentators suggest that this was David's idea to begin with, in order to eliminate Saul's descendants who might become rivals for the throne of Israel. Brueggemann suggests that this account "serves primarily to give David warrant for his violence against the house of Saul" (*First and Second Samuel,* 337).

5. Burlap.

6. Rizpah's vigil probably lasts several months, from March/April to October. See Alter, *The David Story,* 331; Mellish, *1 & 2 Samuel,* 274.

7. See 1 Samuel 20:12-17, 42.

8. The tragedy and the agony of Rizpah have been captured in "The Vigil of Rizpah," a poem by Felicia Dorothea Hemans. http://www.poetry explorer.net/poem.php?id=10070438. Last accessed September 29, 2015.

Chapter 21

1. The designation "son of Jehoiada" distinguishes this Benaiah from the Benaiah cited in 1 Chronicles 15:16-25 and 16:4-6, from the Benaiah listed in 1 Chronicles 4:36, and from "Benaiah the Pirathonite" listed among the Thirty (see 2 Samuel 23:30, 1 Chronicles 11:31, and 27:14).

2. See 2 Samuel 23:20-22; 1 Chronicles 11:22-24.

3. For an excellent treatment of this episode, see Mark Batterson, *In a Pit with a Lion on a Snowy Day* (Nashville: Multnomah, 2006).

4. Literally, "like a weaver's rod," which is a long, wooden shaft used in a loom. See 1 Samuel 17:7; 2 Samuel 22:19; 1 Chronicles 11:23; 20:5.

5. See 2 Samuel 8:18; 20:23.

6. See 1 Chronicles 11:25; 2 Samuel 23:23.

7. See 1 Chronicles 27:5-6.

8. "A last will and testament worthy of a dying Mafia capo" is how Robert Alter describes David's final words to his son and successor. *The David Story,* 374.

9. Readers interested in the story of Benaiah and David's mighty warriors should reference *Day of War: Lion of War Series,* by Cliff Graham (Grand Rapids: Zondervan, 2011). Graham's fascinating, fictional account fleshes out the story of Benaiah and the lion, as well as the exploits of the Three, highlighting battle tactics as well as providing cultural and contextual details.

10. This quote is widely attributed to Frank Boreham.

Afterword

1. John Wesley, *Explanatory Notes Upon The New Testament: Volume 1* (Peabody, MA: Hendrickson Publishers, Inc., 1986), notes on Acts 13:22.

2. See Psalm 78:72.